The Voice Exercise Book

Jeannette Nelson

The Voice Exercise Book

A Guide to Healthy
and Effective Voice Use

National
Theatre

National Theatre Publishing

PUBLISHED BY
NATIONAL THEATRE PUBLISHING
The Royal National Theatre,
South Bank, London SE1 9PX
www.nationaltheatre.org.uk

First published 2015

The author is not a health practitioner
and does not purport to give medical
advice. If a reader is in any doubt as to
whether to adopt any recommendation
made in this book on account of an
existing medical condition or health
concern, they should seek advice from
a health practitioner.

*A catalogue record for this book is
available from the British Library*

Printed and bound in the United Kingdom
by Cantate Communications
Design and illustrations by Tal Brosh

Distributed by Nick Hern Books
The Glasshouse, 49a Goldhawk Road,
London W12 8QP
www.nickhernbooks.co.uk

ISBN 978-1-84842-654-2 paperback

To my teachers, David Carey and Patsy Rodenberg

**Watch Jeannette Nelson coaching
on iTunes U and YouTube**

A series of free online videos from the National Theatre are available to complement the material in this book. These videos are available on YouTube (www.youtube.com/ntdiscovertheatre) and iTunes U (https://itun.es/i6Bv9gt#iTunes). Each short film has a different area of focus: a vocal warm-up; a demonstration of how an actor engages the voice to fill different theatrical spaces (using the three stages in the National Theatre); and a series of exercises with texts that Jeannette would typically use in rehearsals, with a particular emphasis on Shakespeare.

Contents

Preface

I feel extremely lucky to have written this book while working at the National Theatre. In this wonderful institution there are many unseen and unsung heroes. Some of these dedicated and busy people found time to help me.

Alice King-Farlow said yes to the book in the first place, and Katie Town provided early support and encouragement. Kathryn Marten, Emma Gosden, Paula Hamilton and Kate Godfrey, my dear colleague in the voice department, all read the manuscript and gave advice. Ollie Winser provided the art direction and Kate Bone published the book.

However, some of the most important contributors to the book are from outside the National Theatre. Matthew Mills cast his expert eye over the scientific and medical elements. The delightful illustrations and design are the work of Tal Brosh, using Tondi Mpambawashe as her model for the male drawings. Finally, Kathryn Perry was my brilliant, patient and understanding editor, who really made the book what it is.

My grateful thanks to you all.

Foreword

Everyone knows that actors need to be comprehensible, and everyone knows that they need to be truthful. All actors know how much of a challenge it is to be both.

Jeannette Nelson is at the heart of the National Theatre's rehearsal process. She gives actors the confidence to embrace the vast auditorium of the Olivier Theatre, and she knows how to make them believe that through the exercise of their imaginations and the relentless exercise of their craft they can hit the back wall at the same time as they exchange the most delicate intimacies with their fellow actors.

Jeannette seems to me to be absolutely devoted to the idea that you can't be real on stage without letting the audience in. If you aren't skilled enough to communicate what you're saying, thinking and feeling, you are by definition untruthful, because truth in the theatre doesn't exist in a vacuum. If the audience doesn't know what's going on, nothing's going on. And nothing is neither truthful nor untruthful – it's nothing.

Through Jeannette's work, and through the craft that she teaches, actors learn that technique and truth are bedfellows, and that vocal projection isn't just a matter of speaking loud enough; it's the consequence of a fully engaged imagination.

She and I have worked together countless times on Shakespeare's plays, and I've learned an enormous amount from her. We agree that it's possible to speak Shakespeare's lines as if they are the spontaneous consequence of a real thought process, and that you can do this without compromising how extraordinary they are.

Every year, actors at the National become better actors because they've worked with Jeannette. This book shows why.

Nicholas Hytner
London 2015

Introduction

This book is for anyone who wants to use their voice more effectively. It is designed to be a simple and straightforward guide to good voice production, beginning with an explanation of how the voice works and followed by exercises to establish a reliable vocal technique.

I have developed this work over the many years I have been working as a theatre voice coach at Britain's National Theatre, the Royal Shakespeare Company and at Shakespeare's Globe. I have used, and continue to use, these exercises to train and keep in shape the voices of all types of actors. I take the same approach with experienced and well-known actors as I do with those at the beginning of their careers.

I also use the work with people who are not in the theatre. We can all improve the performance of our voice with knowledge of how it works and by practising simple exercises.

In Chapter 9 you can find out more about how I apply the work at the National Theatre.

Who is this book for?

This book is for actors, teachers and anyone else who uses their voice professionally. That might be all day or just at meetings and presentations, or in the theatre. Its content is based on the work I do every day with professional actors and is therefore suitable for anyone who has to 'perform' with their voice, whether on stage, in school, in a place of worship, in the boardroom, on the sales floor or on the end of a telephone. Being heard and understood, clearly and easily, is of course the desire of all who use their voice to communicate professionally.

You may already have a strong reason for choosing this book. Perhaps you have experienced some difficulties when using your voice professionally or have been advised that improving your verbal communication skills will advance your career. Maybe you have to speak for extended periods or have to use enough volume to fill a big space and command an audience. Or you may need your voice to show confidence and authority when speaking at meetings, selling your products or dealing with the public.

You may be an actor who wants to keep their voice in shape, or who wants an effective warm-up routine.

You may be a teacher whose voice gets tired after a day in the classroom, or who wants to help your students develop their voices for theatre performances. You could have a physical condition that affects your voice, or maybe you just have a sense that you are not getting the best out of it.

Whatever your reason, the exercises in this book teach you the techniques required for good, healthy voice use and clear speaking in all circumstances. Whatever your starting point, you have the ability to enhance your voice and use it well.

How to use the book

An authentic voice

Before beginning to work with the exercises, it is important to spend a little time thinking about your voice: what it means to you and what it says about you.

The principles of using your voice well are the same for everyone and they are very simple. You have to breathe freely and deeply, and then allow the resonant voice out of your body through clearly articulated speech. This book will teach you how to do that.

However, it is not enough if the sound of your voice doesn't ring true. Whatever your reason for wanting to work on your voice, your aim should be authenticity. Believe me, you will not engage your listeners fully or feel truly satisfied with your voice unless it sounds authentic – honestly yours. A healthy, expressive voice is not achieved by affecting a way of speaking or copying someone else. It is achieved by developing the voice you have.

So in Chapter 1 I ask you to consider your voice as unique; coming from your body and your personality, and being influenced, like the rest of you, by your personal experiences. This is where I begin with actors and with non-actors. You first have to get to know your voice and how it works before you can develop its potential.

I also ask you to consider how you use your voice and the way you speak in order to present yourself to the world. I don't ask you to judge this but to recognise that it says a great deal about you – who you are and how you think. Through this process you might come to understand why your verbal communication isn't always as good as it could be. Then you can begin to make changes.

How your voice works

The next stage is to learn how your voice works physically, so there follows a short explanation of the anatomy and physiology of the voice. There's nothing too complex here; just a hands-on exploration of all the parts of the body that work together to produce your voice. Understanding how breath and voice work is the key to getting to know your voice.

Once you understand how your voice works you need to know how to look after it. I therefore end this chapter with some information and advice on continued voice care.

So you begin by getting to know the voice you have, and then go on to learn how it works and how to look after it. All of this is designed to heighten your self-awareness in preparation for the vocal technique exercises.

Voice exercises

Chapters 2 and 3 contain the voice exercises. The first group in Chapter 2 teach you, or remind you, of the basics of voice training: breath, resonance, opening the voice and articulation. This is the foundation for all your work.

You can also see these exercises demonstrated in a series of free online videos from the National Theatre. These videos are available on YouTube (www.youtube.com/ntdiscovertheatre) and iTunes U

WE CAN ALL IMPROVE THE PERFORMANCE OF OUR VOICE BY KNOWING HOW IT WORKS AND BY PRACTISING SIMPLE EXERCISES.

(https://itun.es/i6Bv9gt#iTunes). Each short film has a different area of focus: a vocal warm-up; a demonstration of how an actor engages the voice to fill different theatrical spaces (using the three stages in the National Theatre); and a series of exercises that I would typically use in rehearsals, with a particular emphasis on Shakespeare.

When you are comfortable and familiar with the exercises in Chapter 2 and feel that your voice is developing, you can go on to the exercises in Chapter 3, which build on this foundation. These will deepen your knowledge and expand your technique, leading to more freedom, control and variety of expression. There are also exercises to help you speak loudly or shout without tiring your voice.

Working with the exercises is intended to be progressive. Regular repetition will develop control of the breath; enhance the quality, clarity and power of the sound; and increase your sense of ownership of your voice. You will see that the exercises encourage you to feel your voice more than listen to it. People often get frustrated when their voice doesn't work the way they want it to, and this is partly because they can't see it or touch it. Understanding how it works and developing a kinaesthetic awareness is vital. Then you can self-monitor and self-correct.

Chapter 4 helps you with the demands of performance, whether or not that is on stage, teaching you how to warm up and warm down. In Chapter 5 I look at particular voice problems that might affect you, and suggest which exercises you should focus on to help you overcome them.

Beyond the basics

If you are an actor or other type of performer, you may wish to continue working with this book to develop a lifelong practice. If you work in other professions, you may find that once you have explored how your voice works and learned to breathe and speak effectively, you will use the techniques naturally in everyday life. You could then return to the book from time to time to refresh your work or if a particular need arises.

Communicating well with your voice is essential to getting your message across. So in Chapter 6 I have included some exercises for those of you who wish to make your accent clearer. Then in Chapter 7 I point out some common communication problems, and advise on how to overcome them in order to keep your audience listening and interested.

For those of you who teach drama in schools and colleges or youth theatre groups, I have also included a chapter on working with young people's voices. Young people gain many life skills from experiencing the creative force of making theatre. Finding confidence in their voices and communicating with them well are among the most important of these skills. However, working with young adults whose voices, bodies and minds are still developing needs a particular focus and care. When I work with this group I tailor the exercises to meet their needs and abilities, and in Chapter 8 I share some of these with you.

Falling in love with your voice

An important part of working with these exercises is that you will build a relationship with your voice. As you practise the exercises, you will get to know your voice and body well. You will think about your posture, and touch your body to feel the movement of breathing and the vibration of your voice. You will listen to your voice and breath to hear how they change, and you will feel them inside your body. This relationship will be for life. You will gradually find that good breathing and the effective release of voice and speech become a habit. You will learn to recognise the things that hinder the voice and have ways to remove or overcome them.

I often think that we should fall in love with our voice. We should get to know it well, and then nurture and support it, and help it to grow. This is what these exercises are designed to do.

So don't be intimidated; dive in and try them. It's your voice and you can learn to use it well.

WE SHOULD FALL IN LOVE WITH OUR VOICE. WE SHOULD GET TO KNOW IT WELL, AND THEN NURTURE AND SUPPORT IT, AND HELP IT TO GROW.

1.

Getting to know your voice

THERE IS NO VOICE
WITHOUT BREATH.

What your voice says about you

There is no mystery about the mechanics of the human voice. It is a physical activity, and, like all physical activities, if you want to perform well you have to practise and develop your technique. However, the voice is an expression of self like no other, and as such is subject to inner feelings and outward pressures.

Who you are

Our voice is part of our identity and it carries our history. It tells where we are from through our accent or language, tying us to place and community. That might be very important to us, and we may take pride in the accent and dialect that identifies us with the history of a particular place and group of people.

Our voice is also one of the ways we choose to engage with the world. We may use volume, speaking loudly to show that we are confident and in control, or quietly, making people listen closely. We may use tone to project a particular image of ourselves: maybe caring or careless, firm or ironic. We may use our voice to protect ourselves and hide behind, perhaps by changing our native accent, or pushing or withholding its natural energy. We may also enhance the expression of our gender by using a rather high or low pitch.

Authenticity

If you are unhappy with the way you sound and have tried to change it on your own, you may be surprised to know that people usually realise that something is not quite right. We recognise authenticity when we hear it and mistrust those whose voices don't quite fit them. I'm sure you have listened to people in public life who you feel are not using their voices honestly or authentically, and you don't trust them.

The work in this book is not about forcing the voice to sound different. It is about getting to know the voice you have and working with it. Actors need to know themselves well, and be comfortable and honest about who they are, before they can transform themselves into other people. They aim to reveal truths in the world, and to do so they have to work from a place of authenticity. Voice training is an essential part of this as it teaches them how to discover and release their true voice. Then they can get to know it well and fully own it.

This is what I hope to offer you. The exercises teach you how to feel the breath and the voice within your own body, and then how to maximise its potential for expression and communication. That doesn't mean it won't change. If you work with proper care, of course your voice will change but it will still sound like you. In fact, it may sound more like you than it did before, because you will have released it fully. It will be a sound with more resonance, more range, more flexibility and more honesty.

How you feel

The voice is also a means of expressing emotion, and it is often our first response to the things that life brings us: we laugh and cry, and we make spontaneous expressive noises – oh, ah, mm, argh. Our voice can also reveal how we feel even when we don't mean it to. We know when a friend is not in their usual state of mind, not necessarily by what they say but by how they sound. Unhappiness and anxiety tend to take the music out of the voice, which in turn can make the speaker try to force energy into it in an attempt to disguise their feelings. Insecurity and fear can lead to physical tensions that create a thin, high, husky or quiet voice.

But when we are happy our bodies relax. We can breathe deeply and freely, so the voice can be comfortable and natural. A natural voice is what we are aiming for in this book: a voice that is clear, resonant, unstrained and easy to listen to. And most important of all, we are aiming for a voice that reflects who we truly are. When working at its best, it will respond to our thinking without effort and with a full range of expression.

How others respond to your voice

The voice can also be something that is judged by others. As children we were often told to be quiet or not to say things. As adults we recognise that some types of accent or speech are more valued than others. These criticisms, if excessive or inappropriate, can lead to vocal difficulties, especially when we need to use our voice in public or professional situations.

If you learn early on that you are supposed to keep quiet, you may come to believe that what you have to say is not important. This can lead to a habit of speaking too fast or too softly, or even to being reluctant to speak at all. If you think your accent or speaking style is unacceptable, it can stop you from breathing adequately for speech. Any criticism of how you speak can lead to holding tension in your jaw, throat or shoulders.

However, a little knowledge and technique can bring about a healthier and more satisfying relationship with your voice. Then the confidence that this creates helps to overcome the external pressures that can make speaking hard. This does not happen instantly: you do have to do the exercises and absorb the technique. But learning to control your voice, owning it and falling in love with it will help you to develop self-confidence. You will find that people will want to listen to you. Think of it as regaining what should be naturally yours.

Summary

— Think about your voice and what it says about you.
  What does it say about where you are from?
— Does it show how you feel and how you feel about
  yourself? Are you trying to hide behind it?
— Are you trying to force it to sound different?
— Allow yourself to fall in love with the voice you have. This
  book will show you how to nurture it and help it to grow.

How your voice works – breathing

Have you ever thought about how you breathe? And have you ever thought about the relationship between breathing and speaking? What about when you get out of breath and can't speak properly? Other than that, you probably haven't really needed to think about breath and voice if they are working perfectly well together. It is only when we have to put extra demands on the breath – chairing a meeting, working all day on the telephone, teaching, preaching or acting – that it needs a bit of attention. There is no voice without breath.

Sit quietly and notice the feeling of your body breathing. You are probably most aware of the air coming in and out of your nose. That's how we breathe quietly to stay alive. When we need to use the breath more vigorously we usually breathe through our mouths – think of running or doing an exercise class. It's quicker to get bigger breaths in through the mouth. The same goes for speaking, when we also need more air than simply to stay alive. So we usually breathe in through our mouths when we speak.

However, many of us don't take enough breath to enable the voice to work effectively and healthily when speaking for long periods. To keep your voice working well you need to breathe deeply. As you sit and notice your breath, do you feel some movement around your waist and stomach? That's your diaphragm moving to allow the air to go down into the bottom of your lungs (I'll tell you more about that later in this chapter). If you don't feel this and only feel some movement in your upper chest, then your breathing is called 'shallow'. The work in this book will help you to lower your breathing and so find more freedom and power in your voice.

If this is the first time you have thought about how you breathe, you may suddenly feel that it is hard work or that you are taking in bigger breaths than you need at present. These feelings will pass. As you work through the book, your awareness of your breathing mechanism will start to put you in control and you will develop a natural and easy pattern of deep breathing.

How your breathing affects your listener

We have a tendency to mirror a person we are listening to. If their voice sounds tight in their throat, we begin to tighten our own. If their breathing is shallow, we begin to feel tight in the chest. When they don't take enough time to breathe for speaking, we don't get enough time to digest what they're saying.

In everyday speech it is usual to breathe in when we have a new thought or idea. But the anxiety of speaking in formal situations can interfere with this instinct and leave us without enough breath to speak easily. By becoming aware of the connection between thinking, breathing and speaking, and then allowing it to happen effortlessly, your listeners will understand you better and feel more comfortable.

The breath gives a fresh energy to what you are about to say, and this stimulates your listeners' interest. This is true of all speaking, including reading aloud. You will not lose your listeners' interest if you take enough time for breath. On the contrary, if they cannot follow your thoughts because they are rushing one on top of the other, they will quickly lose interest in what you are saying.

Breathing in is also an action that can release throat tension. If you feel that your throat is getting tight, consciously take the opportunity to release it as you take in your next breath. Try that now. Let your mouth drop open a little (we usually breathe in through the mouth when we are speaking) and see if you can let your throat relax.

It might help to focus the release on the very back of your tongue where it goes down into your throat. It might also help to gently stroke down the front of your neck with the forefinger and thumb, starting under the chin. Can you feel that? If so, you are beginning to feel how you can make physical changes that affect the way you use your voice.

How your breath works

The lungs are pear-shaped: they are larger at the bottom than at the top. They are encased in the rib cage, which has 24 ribs – 12 on each side. The top seven pairs are attached to the spine at the back and

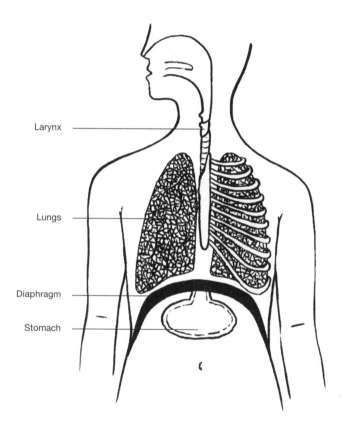

Larynx

Lungs

Diaphragm

Stomach

the breastbone at the front. These are called the 'true ribs'. The next three pairs are not attached directly to the breastbone but linked to it and to each other by cartilage. These are known as the 'false ribs'. The final two pairs are attached to the spine at the back and not to the breastbone at all. These are known as the 'floating ribs'. Because the false ribs and the floating ribs are not fixed to the breastbone, they are able to move more easily as the bottom of the lungs fill with air.

Attached all around the bottom edge of the rib cage is the diaphragm. It is a flexible, dome-shaped sheet of muscle that divides the body in half, being the floor of the chest and the ceiling of the abdomen (it is not just at the front of the body).

Touch it

Using the fingers of both hands, find the bottom of your breastbone. It is quite high up, isn't it? Now walk your fingertips around the bottom of your rib cage on each side, going right around to the back until your hands meet at the spine. You have now walked your fingers around the edge of your diaphragm. When you breathe in, the diaphragm lowers and pushes all the abdominal organs down and slightly forward. You have probably heard that actors control their voices by breathing into their stomach or abdomen. Well, it is this action that gives that sensation and control.

When breathing for singing or for the sustained and powerful voice you need when speaking on stage or in a large room, the rib cage widens to help to give more space for air entering the lungs. However, this action should happen most strongly in the lower ribs, not at the top of the rib cage.

Try it

See if you can feel this as you breathe in: the ribs at the waist widening and the abdomen coming forward a little. If this doesn't happen, the breath is probably just filling your upper chest – the shallow breathing I mentioned earlier. Try taking a really big breath. What happens? Do you feel your chest rising and your shoulders coming up? If you do, then this is not a useful breath to speak with. Even if you are only taking a small breath, this action pushes your chest up against your larynx and restricts the throat and the action of the tongue.

What about your stomach and your abdominal area? Were you holding it tight and flat? If you are sitting down, your abdominal muscles are probably relaxed. Stand up. Do you automatically pull your stomach in? Let it go and try the deep breath again. You should now be able to feel the movement of the diaphragm into your abdomen.

Letting the abdominal muscles relax can be very difficult. Socially, many of us feel we are supposed to be slim, especially in this area. Often when we are under pressure or feel afraid, we have an instinct to tighten our muscles so that we are ready for action. Physical exercise teachers may have encouraged you to tighten these muscles to increase your core strength. For whatever reason, holding may have become a habit. However, if you really want your voice to reach its full potential, then you have to let go of your abdominal muscles.

The breathing exercises in Chapters 2 and 3 will help you to lower your breathing.

Summary

- Take some time to explore what happens in your body as you breathe. Get familiar with your diaphragm and how your ribs move.
- Practise letting your abdominal muscles relax so that you can breathe deeply and effectively.
- When speaking in public, let your breath come in with each new thought or idea. Your listener will understand you better.

How your voice works – making sound

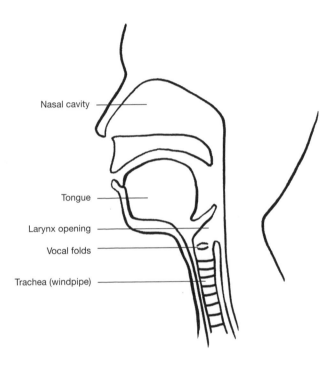

Nasal cavity

Tongue

Larynx opening

Vocal folds

Trachea (windpipe)

When you speak you are breathing air out of your lungs. Voice happens as the vocal folds in your throat vibrate the air passing through them on its way out of the body. This vibrating air is sound, which then travels on up through the throat and into your mouth, where words are formed.

When you have an idea of something to say you breathe in. You speak as you breathe out.

The vocal folds are situated in the larynx behind the Adam's apple. They are a group of muscles (so no longer called the vocal 'cords') that vibrate the air passing through them to make sound. Above them is a space that is the first amplifier of the sound made at the vocal folds. After passing through this space the sound is also amplified in the mouth and nasal sinuses.

Even women have an Adam's apple, although it is not as noticeable as a man's. Explore the front of your neck with your fingers to feel your larynx. It's that flexible column of cartilage in your throat. Do you feel the knobbly point of your Adam's apple in the centre? If you hum a little, you will feel the vibrations of the vocal folds within it. Can you feel the vibrations all the way up to your chin? You might even feel them in your face and nose.

How tension restricts your voice

It is very easy for the throat space to be restricted. Try tightening your shoulders a little. Do you feel that in your throat? Bite your back teeth together. Feel that in your throat? Tighten the corners of your mouth. Feel that in your throat? All of these tensions constrict the throat space, and the spaces in the mouth and nose are also compromised. If you carry any of that tension habitually, your voice will get tired as you struggle to release it, especially when you need to speak loudly and for long periods. So you can see how important it is to let go of tension in the areas that affect the throat.

How posture affects your voice

Anxiety can cause you to tighten in these areas, but bad posture is one of the main reasons for the vocal apparatus to become constricted. If I ask you where you carry your tension, I guess you would probably say in your shoulders or neck. Most of us do.

Take a moment to think about how you normally sit. If you are working at a desk or computer all day, is your back rounded? Do you sit with your chest collapsed, squashing your stomach and diaphragm? Is your head tilted back to see the screen, and therefore pressing down on the back of your neck?

What about when you are standing? Stand up now and think about your normal posture. Or better still, have a look in a full-length mirror.

Do you hold your shoulders hunched or rounded? Is your chest collapsed now? Do you push your hips forward or do you do the opposite, arching your back and pushing your chest up?

All of these postural habits can cause tension in the neck, shoulders and throat. They can also restrict the free flow of your breath. But these tensions and constrictions can be relieved by making sure you are standing up tall, with your neck as an extension of your spine. Round shoulders put a lot of strain on your neck and lower back.

Summary

— Enjoy the feeling of your voice vibrating in your throat.
  We speak as we breathe out.
— Try to become aware of habitual tensions in your
  shoulders, jaw and mouth as these interfere with
  your voice.
— Remember to stand up tall. Good posture is an important
  part of voice work.

How your voice works – making words

Speaking clearly

When the vibrating voice enters the mouth it is articulated into speech by the action of the tongue, lips and jaw (the articulators). The tension I talked about in the areas surrounding the face and neck will also inhibit the free movement of the articulators in speech. So the more freedom you have to move the articulators, the more variety you will find in your range of expression.

A clear and easy speaking style does not involve pushing in any way. My aim for you is that the sound of your voice and the clarity of your speech are never forced. Your listeners should be listening to what you are saying, not how you say it.

> **Clear speech comes from release not effort**
> If you put too much effort into the actions of articulating speech, you are likely to tense the muscles and close down the acoustic spaces in the throat, nose and mouth. This will result in strain. When you speak you should aim to have space between your teeth. This gives room for your tongue to move freely.

Consonants

Consonant sounds are very important in clear speech and they are made with the lips and the tongue. The tongue is incredibly dexterous. It moves very quickly between consonants using the tip, the sides and the back. These moves happen more easily when there is enough space in the mouth. Then the sounds are clearer.

In the exercises I sometimes ask you to make consonant sounds. Although I use letters of the alphabet like **T**, **D** or **Y** to write the sounds, these letters represent the [t] sound at the beginning of the word 'tell', the [d] sound at the beginning of the word 'day' or the [y] sound at the beginning of the word 'yacht'.

Try the sounds **T**, **D**, **L**, **N**, **S**, **Z**, **R**, **TH**. These are some of the consonants made with the tip of the tongue. Try **Y**: this is made with the sides of the tongue. **K**, **G**, **NG** are made with the back of the tongue. The consonants made with the lips are **B**, **P**, **W, M**. The consonants made with the lips and teeth are **V**, **F**. When there is more space in the mouth the lips also work more freely and with more energy.

In Chapters 2 and 3 I provide some articulation exercises, including tongue twisters. These exercises use the repetition of different consonants to train the muscles of the tongue and the lips to produce clear and accurate sounds.

Summary

— Remember, clear speech comes from release not effort. Are you aware of forcing your voice rather than releasing its natural energy?
— Make sure you have enough space between your top and bottom teeth for your tongue to move quickly, freely and accurately between consonants. This will help you to speak clearly.
— Consonants are made with the tip, the sides and the back of the tongue, and with the lips. Try out consonant sounds made with these different areas.

A NATURAL VOICE IS WHAT WE
ARE AIMING FOR: A VOICE THAT
IS CLEAR, RESONANT, UNSTRAINED
AND EASY TO LISTEN TO.

Looking after your voice

Like any other part of your body, your voice needs to be fed, exercised and looked after.

Staying hydrated

Most important of all, your voice needs to be watered. If you use your voice for long periods of time, the vocal folds will lose moisture. The mucus that covers them and allows them to move easily against each other will then thicken. This stops them from vibrating properly and they could become damaged. When you stay hydrated, the mucus is thin and slippery, and keeps the vocal folds vibrating smoothly.

It is recommended that we drink one-and-a-half to two litres of water every day. Try drinking one small glass of water (about 125 ml) an hour. This hydrates the vocal folds from the inside, and I guarantee that you will feel less tired, both vocally and physically.

You can also hydrate the vocal folds from the outside by steaming with hot water. You can do this breathing over a bowl of hot water with a towel over your head, or you can buy a cosmetic or medical steamer from a chemist or pharmacy. It is recommended that you steam when you are using your voice strenuously or have a chest or throat infection. Steam once in the morning and once again at night, or, if you have to perform, about an hour before you begin. Do not add anything to the water.

A healthy diet

For a healthy voice you need a healthy body. As recommended by doctors and dieticians, you should eat a well-balanced diet and take regular physical exercise. However, there are certain foods and drinks that do have an adverse effect on the voice and should be taken in moderation.

Caffeine and alcohol have diuretic properties and therefore take water out of your body. You should modify your intake of these or make sure you drink plenty of water with them.

Dairy produce can create the excess mucus called catarrh. So if you have a cold or infection, or if you feel your voice just isn't working well, you could consider reducing your dairy consumption.

If your throat feels sore in the mornings and your voice regularly sounds hoarse, you may have acid reflux. This means that digestive juices are coming up from your stomach into your throat and affecting your vocal folds. It is a condition that can be brought on by eating spicy or fatty foods and drinking fizzy drinks. It may also be caused by eating too close to going to bed – something common among actors who work in the evening. However, these symptoms can also indicate other medical conditions, so always seek advice from a doctor.

Irritants

Smoking any substances will seriously dry the vocal folds and adversely affect lung function. A prolonged smoking habit can cause the voice to become deep, rasping and difficult to project. Smoke damages the lungs, causing persistent coughing, and the breath capacity of the lungs is also restricted.

Aspirin (and analgesics that contain aspirin) can increase the possibility of a vocal fold haemorrhage because of their anti-coagulant properties. Do not take or gargle with any aspirin products when you have a vocal problem.

Inhalers for asthma and other lung conditions should be used with a spacer (you can buy one from a chemist or pharmacy). A spacer is a large plastic or metal container with a mouthpiece at one end and a hole at the other for your aerosol inhaler. It delivers the medicine directly to your lungs, which helps prevent the medicine from irritating your mouth and throat. Make sure you rinse out your mouth with water after using your inhaler.

Resting your voice

Voice rest is crucial if you have any vocal strain – and by rest I mean absolute silence, preferably for a day or two. Don't whisper instead of speaking as this can put more strain on vocal folds that are tired. If you have to keep speaking for your job, be silent when you can. If you take an extended period of voice rest or lose your voice, be sure to warm up properly before you have to speak again professionally.

Summary

- Make sure you drink plenty of water. This is essential for a healthy and efficient voice.
- A healthy, balanced diet will support a healthy voice. Are you taking substances that dry or irritate the voice? Can you modify your use of these or cut them out completely?
- Resting your voice with silence will help it to recover from strain. Don't forget to warm up your voice before you have to speak again professionally.

2.

Voice exercises
– stage 1

THE RELEASE OF PHYSICAL TENSION WILL
RELEASE THE POWER OF YOUR VOICE.

The exercises in this chapter will teach you to breathe deeply and freely to supply your voice. They will enable you to improve the resonance, open out the sound effectively and prepare your mouth to speak words clearly. You can use them to warm up your voice, and if you repeat them over time they will improve your vocal technique.

If you are a theatrical performer, you should warm up your voice before every performance. At the National Theatre the actors warm up about an hour before they perform. If you are a teacher or in any other profession that requires you to use your voice for sustained periods, I suggest you warm up in the mornings. When you know the exercises well, you will be able to do that quite quickly. If you are particularly rushed, you may even find you can warm up as you travel to work. You could do a longer warm up if you have a special speaking event.

Remember, this sort of voice use is athletic, and no athlete would dream of exercising their sport without warming up.

I usually spend 15 to 20 minutes on a warm-up with actors at the National Theatre. However, an actor might do a physical warm-up as well, and on average take about 30 minutes to warm up for performance. Chapter 4 provides you with a concise voice warm-up based on the exercises in Chapter 2.

You may want to build a repertoire of exercises that you find useful from this chapter and from Chapter 3, especially if you are a theatrical performer. Or you may just need to understand how to use your voice effectively in your everyday life. If this is the case, then it will probably be enough to work through the exercises in this chapter until your body has established good habits of breath and speech.

When to do voice exercises

You can do your voice practice at any time that is convenient to you. You could do your exercises every day or once or twice a week, depending on how quickly you wish to change your habits of speech. To begin with you will need enough time to understand and absorb the techniques. But you will soon know them well enough to be able to do them easily, especially when you have read and understood how breathing and speaking work in the body.

At the end of this chapter you will find a checklist to use just before you give your presentation or go into your classroom or on to the stage. The concise warm-up in Chapter 4 will also be useful when you know the exercises well.

You can also see these exercises demonstrated in a series of free online videos from the National Theatre. These videos are available at YouTube (www.youtube.com/ntdiscovertheatre) and iTunesU (https://itun.es/i6Bv9gt#iTunes).

Once you have prepared your body, the exercises fall into four sections: breath, resonance, opening the voice and articulation.

Preparation – stretches, posture and abdominal release

Stretches
Stretching the upper body releases the shoulder joints, opens up the rib cage and realigns posture. Allow yourself to really enjoy the following stretch.

Stand with your feet hip-width apart.

Hold your arms out in front of you and take hold of one wrist with the other hand. Now gently pull the arm that you are holding away from you until you feel your shoulder joint and your ribs stretching out.

Change the direction of the pull a little to move the area of stretch. Then pull your arm up above your head, down towards the ground and then to either side. Stretch out of the shoulder joints, waist and pelvis.

Change the direction and angle of the stretch whenever you wish, and you can change hands at any time.

Stand up straight again with your feet hip-width apart.

Posture and abdominal release

Flop over forward from the waist and hang loose with your knees bent. Let your neck be loose and your head hang down.

Breathe deeply and notice how the movement of your breath widens your rib cage across your lower back. Allow your abdomen to relax, and feel it move with your breath against the top of your thighs.

Roll up as if you are rebuilding your spine, vertebra by vertebra, and see if you can stay connected to the feeling of breathing into your relaxed abdomen. Try not to raise your chest, shoulders or chin as you come up.

When you are standing up again, make sure your knees are not locked back. Keep them soft. Locking your knees sends tension right through your body and will lock your breath.

Be aware of the weight of your feet on the floor.
Breathe down into your abdomen.

This is a way to centre yourself.

It is useful to flop over from the waist at any time you feel tired or if you are losing your connection with your deep breathing. It releases your shoulders, neck and abdomen, and sends blood to your brain. So when you roll up again and centre yourself, you feel refreshed and find it easier to breathe.

Breath – breathing deeply to support your voice

Breathing deeply

These breathing exercises teach you to breathe deeply without tension in your neck, shoulders and chest. They also help you to develop the capacity of your breath.

They begin by using the consonant sound **S** that is just a breath sound. Then they move on to the **Z** sound – a vibrating sound – and finally into words.

If you can, squat down. In this position you can feel your breath go even deeper into your body until you feel as if you are breathing right down into your bottom.

With the movement of your breath you can also feel a 'barrel of breathing' around your pelvic girdle and lower ribs. This is where all the powerful breathing muscles are.

If you prefer, you could sit on a chair and flop forward over your knees. You should feel the same movement and depth of breath.

Slowly roll up again, keeping the sense of breathing into your pelvis and keeping your abdomen soft.

It is possible that when you first begin to breathe very deeply you may feel an emotional response. Try not to worry about this or inhibit it. I have already spoken of how physical tensions interfere with the free release of breath and voice, and I am sure you are aware that habitual physical tensions are often a reaction to the challenges that life throws at us. Our protective instincts are very powerful.

Sometimes these physical tensions might hold the memory of difficult, perhaps traumatic events. If these do surface, you must make sure you receive any support you need. More usually, though, our body is just relieved when we let go, and this can be expressed as tears. When it happened to me it was a joyful experience. So you might cry, you might laugh or you might just breathe, but I assure you that whatever your response, it is the release of physical tension that will release the power of your voice.

Supporting your voice

When you are using effective breathing for speaking it is known as 'support'. Exercises 1 and 2 will teach you how to support your voice with your breath, and they are the exercises that begin every voice warm up. They are designed to create a steady stream of air to vibrate your vocal folds.

You can do the following breathing exercises in any comfortable position: standing, sitting, squatting or lying on your back. Lying on your back is a good position to begin with, as your abdominal muscles are relaxed and you feel their movement very freely when you breathe. It is best to lie with your feet flat on the ground so that your knees are bent and pointing up. This allows your lower back to open more than when you are standing. You can change position whenever you like. Don't be uncomfortable.

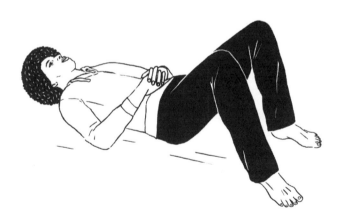

Exercise 1: Organising your breathing muscles to support your voice

This exercise will help you to feel the breath carrying sound steadily through your body, supported from deep in your abdomen.

——

Massage the joint of the jaws in front of your earlobes with your fingertips. You may feel this release into your throat. Massage your face, hairline and back of neck. Relax your jaw and let your top teeth separate from the bottom teeth.

Breathe in and make a long, slow, sustained **S**. When you run out of breath, allow the muscles that have contracted as your breath goes out to release so you can breathe in again. Repeat the slow **S**. Release, breathe in and repeat the slow **S**.

Then repeat the exercise using a **Z**. You will probably feel the vibrations of the **Z** right down into your abdomen. Enjoy this feeling. It means you are supporting your voice. Breathe in and make a long, slow, sustained **Z**. Release, breathe in and repeat the slow **Z**. Release, breathe in and repeat the slow **Z**.

That's three breaths for each sound.

——

These sounds should be slow and steady, with a little space over the back of your tongue to allow the sound to flow easily.

You should feel your ribs slowly going down as the air leaves your body, and your abdomen coming in at the end to push out the last of the breath. But you should not go so far as to tighten your throat at the end.

Enjoy the breathing in each time. You will feel movement in both your abdomen and your ribs as you allow air into your lungs.

Don't push the sound out; let it flow out steadily. These exercises are designed to organise the breathing muscles and control the breath, not to project the voice.

Imagine the sound travelling up from your abdomen, through your chest and throat, into your mouth and on to the tip of your tongue.

Exercise 2: Speaking from your abdomen and supporting words

Now that you have experienced your breath and the sound of your voice coming from your abdomen, this exercise will help you to feel the breath with words.

As you do this exercise, allow the feeling of your speaking voice to come from your abdomen. You could imagine that your mouth goes right down to there!

Remember, you breathe in so that you have breath to speak with.

———

Breathe in down to your abdomen.
Count to 10 out loud, but not too loudly.
Release and breathe in again.
Count to 11.
Release and breathe in again.
Count to 12.

———

You could continue this as far as you can, but not to the point where you tighten your throat.

Keep the voice steady and with energy – but again, don't push for volume. You should not feel that you are making an effort with your throat. It is just a space for resonance.

More about support

Supporting your voice from your abdomen does not mean pushing the words out with your abdominal muscles.

Support is when the breathing muscles deep in your abdomen are allowed to engage naturally to sustain the airflow, and therefore the voice. If you release the muscles for the in-breath, your body will do the right thing when you speak. You don't have to *make* it work.

Summary

— These breathing exercises are to release slow, sustained sounds. They will help you to achieve a deep support for your voice and extend your breath capacity and control.
— In order to breathe deeply into your abdomen you must allow your abdominal muscles to relax.
— Make sure you practise the exercises without strain or effort in the throat, and don't push or pump from your abdomen.
— Don't try to project your voice yet. Just let it flow out easily.

Resonance – feeling your voice throughout your body

Using humming, we can find the full resonance of the voice by thinking it and feeling it move around the body. This helps to produce a relaxed, authentic voice.

Exercise 3: Finding resonance in different parts of your body

———

Stand with your feet hip-width apart and your weight balanced on the centre of your feet.

Start humming with your lips closed but not pressed together and your teeth apart. While you hum, do all the actions below to stimulate the feeling of resonance through your body. Listen to the sound and you will hear the changes.

Chest
Firmly pat and massage around the chest area. You will probably feel the vibrations in this area quite easily because there isn't much muscle covering the bones of your rib cage.

Lower ribs
Rub and massage the lower ribs at the front and sides. See if you can get a sense of your voice dropping lower into your body. You may not feel the vibrations so much with your hands, but gradually you should be able to hear the difference.

Lower back
Rub, pat and massage the back of your lower ribs and the top of your pelvis. Loosening resonance into your lower back has a very powerful effect on the quality of your voice. Can you hear it? Can you feel it inside you? It helps to create a sound that is full, stable and owned by you.

What is resonance?
Resonance is the vibration of the voice passing through the amplifying spaces of the throat, mouth and nasal sinuses. Secondary resonance can also be felt in the rest of the body, in the bones and muscles. When resonance is travelling freely through the face, throat and body, the sound of the speaking voice becomes richer and fuller. Good, free resonance also contributes to voice projection.

We can encourage this resonance with movement and touch. By massaging, firmly patting and shaking different parts of the body, we release muscle tension and open up the amplifying spaces.

Abdomen
Bounce and shake the humming down into your abdomen. Now you are focusing a long way from your throat. Shaking your voice deep into your body will help you to release any tension that has kept your voice high or light.

Legs and feet
Shake the humming out of each leg and foot. It's good to be thinking right down to your feet.

Spine
Shake and bounce the humming through your spine. Your whole body is the instrument of your voice. Isn't it good to feel resonance vibrating right through it?
You might not feel resonance everywhere at first. But each time you do these exercises you will feel more.

Stand still again.

Face
Drop your head down towards your chest and hum into your face – the forehead, nose and lips. Gravity will help to release the sound.
Lift your head as you hum. Imagine bringing the resonance up too, keeping it forward in your face and then releasing it out into the space ahead.

Move the face muscles around and move your voice around so that you are sliding through different notes.

Head
Hum into the top of your head using a high-pitched, gentle voice. I think of this as your 'child's voice', and it is an important part of your voice. If you exercise it, the lower notes will sound brighter. Imagine that it goes up into the space above you.

────

Exercise 4: Resonance through the whole range of your voice

────

Still humming, slide down slowly and smoothly through your voice from the highest note to the lowest. Don't strain or reach for the high notes. Allow the voice to start the slide quite gently. And don't worry if you hear a jump in the middle of your range. It is quite normal, and I will talk about this again after Exercise 5.
As you slide, gradually think the sound forward and away from you into the distance.

Repeat several times.

After a few slides, try speaking something – you could just count to ten. Is your voice beginning to feel freer? Does it sound more resonant and colourful?

────

Summary

— Hum to feel the resonance of your voice throughout your body. Then think it carefully into different areas of your body, face and head.
— Pat, massage and shake these areas to enhance the resonance. Then slide a hum down to feel resonance through the whole range of your voice, from the highest note to the lowest.

Opening the voice – releasing sound and exploring your range

Now that you have made a strong connection with your low breath support and found the free resonance of your voice, you can begin to open it up.

First, we stretch again.

Rib stretch
Take a wider stance and bend your knees a little.

With your right arm up, stretch over to the left side, with your left arm wrapped around your body to hold the stretched right side.

Drop the top hand on to the top of your head and relax your shoulders.

Breathe a couple of breaths into the stretched side and feel the ribs swinging out. Try dropping the lower arm. You will feel more stretch.

Drop the right shoulder and elbow forward and you will feel the stretch opening up the back of that side of your rib cage. Take a couple of breaths.

Come up, drop your arms and take a breath. You will feel how the ribs move more freely on the stretched side of your body.

Repeat the whole exercise on your other side.

Finally, stand up straight again and bring your feet back in under your hips. Be aware of the movement of the sides of your ribs as you breathe normally.

Throat stretches
Yawning
Yawning is a great way to stretch all the areas involved with speech: the throat, tongue, lips and face muscles. If you

stretch your body in response to the yawn, you will open up the ribs and shoulders as well.

Stifled yawn
Try another yawn but this time don't open your mouth – as if you were trying to stifle the yawn. Do you feel that big stretch at the back of your mouth?

Standing straight again, let the breath fill the sides of your ribs, and be aware of the movement of the diaphragm down into your abdomen.

Exercise 5: Exploring the range

This exercise is to open up your voice using the whole range, from high to low.

———

Breathe in, then release your voice on a long slow **Ha**, sliding from the very top of your range down to the bottom. Don't push up for the high note at the beginning. Take it from that gentle, child's voice you used in Exercise 3.

Repeat as many times as you like, but always choose to breathe into your lower ribs, diaphragm and abdomen first. Send your voice away from you into the distance. Look at a spot across the room and focus the energy of your voice to that point. Try to keep the vocal energy up and out without pushing it.
Choose to keep your throat and mouth open all the way to the end of the sound.

———

You will probably find a noticeable jump between your 'head voice' and your speaking voice. The head voice refers to the highest range of notes that sound quite light and thin (unless you are a trained singer).

It is called your head voice, because we feel these notes resonate more in the head. I sometimes call it your 'child's voice', as it is the voice you used in childhood before your vocal folds developed fully. In men's voices it is called falsetto.

This jump between your head voice and your speaking voice is known as the 'register break' or 'pitch break' and is perfectly normal. It is a change in the muscle action of the vocal folds between the very high part of the voice and the range of notes we use in speech. In some people it is more distinct than in others.

You will be familiar with the sound in teenage boys' voices when they 'break' as their larynx and vocal folds lengthen and thicken, and their voice drops from the child's high voice to the deeper tones of manhood. Women's voices also change at puberty, but it is less noticeable, as the pitch of their voices drops only a little.

The break between our high voice and lower voice remains in adulthood to some degree. Practising this sliding exercise over time may smooth it out but you shouldn't worry if it doesn't. It is a part of the voice that we notice only when voicing or singing through the entire range. In normal speech we don't usually go that high, but the break can appear when we laugh and cry. Some cultures also use it when singing – think of Country and Western, or some Irish folk singing. Passing quickly down and up through the break is also the technique used to yodel.

Summary

— Stretch your rib cage to allow for a free, full breath.
  Stretch your throat with yawns and stifled yawns.
— Open up your voice by sliding down through the range, from top to bottom, on **Ha**.

Articulation – exercising the muscles of your face and tongue

You now need to wake up the muscles of articulation in your mouth to ensure that the words you speak have energy and clarity.

Prepare by giving your face muscles a workout. Scrunch and stretch your face, but be careful not to tighten your neck.

Move your tongue around in your mouth and with the tip explore every corner.

Stick the front of your tongue out of your mouth – just as far as it's comfortable.

Make a point with the tip, then flatten it. Alternate between pointing and flattening a few times.

Make small circles with the tip in both directions.

Make big circles using the whole tongue.

When you have finished, relax the jaw and connect to your breathing.

Exercise 6: Tip of the tongue

Make a rolled **R**, moving around the whole range of your voice.

Make fast, repeated **D** sounds.

Make fast, repeated **T** sounds.

Exercise 7: Sides of the tongue

___

Repeat **yoh yah, yoh yah** several times.

Repeat **red lorry, yellow lorry, red lorry, yellow lorry** several times.

___

Exercise 8: Back of the tongue

___

Open your mouth enough to get two fingers between your teeth, one above the other.
Put the tip of your tongue behind your bottom teeth.
Take your fingers out but keep the space.
Try to move only your tongue at the back and not the jaw.

Make fast, repeated **G** sounds.

Make fast, repeated **K** sounds.

Repeat **kiggley koo, kiggley koo, kiggley kiggley kiggley koo** several times.

___

Exercise 9: Lips

___

Lift your top lip off your top teeth like a sneer, then let it drop down again.
Repeat several times: up and down, up and down.

Now try that with your bottom lip, dropping it down off your bottom teeth. Try not to tighten your neck.
Repeat several times: down and up, down and up.

Now one after the other: lift the top lip then return your lips together. Drop the bottom lip then return your lips together. Top, together, bottom, together, top, together, bottom, together.

Blow air through your lips and enjoy making them flap.

Make motorbike engine sounds with your lips by blowing your voice through them.

Make fast, repeated **B** sounds. Bounce them around the room.

Make fast, repeated **P** sounds. Make them sharp, popping sounds.

Make fast, repeated **W** sounds. Work the lips quite hard.

Make fast, repeated **M** sounds. Enjoy the buzz on the lips.

———

Tongue twisters are always good exercises providing you do them with a relaxed jaw, connected breath and lots of vocal energy. You'll find some tongue twisters in Exercise 28.

Summary

— Exercise your face and tongue muscles (tip, sides and back), and your lips.
— Use fast, repeated consonants to increase dexterity and muscularity. Practise tongue twisters.

Exercise 10: Putting it all together

Now it is time to put the work together. Can you breathe freely and deeply, and use a resonant sound and clear articulation while reading something aloud?

Take a piece of text: perhaps a poem or a section from a novel or newspaper.

Sitting comfortably, read a section aloud as if you were telling it to someone else. As you do so, notice when you breathe. Be sure that your abdominal muscles are relaxed and that you are breathing from there.

Notice particularly when you take quite big breaths and when you take small breaths. At first you may not realise that you are taking these small breaths. But as you become more aware, you will feel that every so often you just release your throat to let a little air in. We take these breaths when the sense of the piece allows or needs. We breathe to make sense of the structure of thoughts and ideas. It is these little breaths that people often forget to take when they are speaking in public. Then they easily run out of breath and strain their voices.

Now read the section again but more loudly, as if the person you are reading to is across the room. Keep breathing from the abdomen.

Did you notice that you took more big breaths and that you took them more regularly? You probably took them at most of the punctuation marks, including commas. You may also have noticed that after you took a new breath your voice had more energy and you sounded more interesting. However, not all breaths have to be very big; they do vary according to what you are going to say. As I said in the introduction, we normally breathe for thought. Small thoughts need smaller breaths than big thoughts.

How about your jaw? Were you able to let it be free so that your tongue could pronounce the words clearly? How about your throat? Did it tighten as you spoke more loudly or were you able to keep it relaxed enough for resonance to come through?

Does it seem as if there are a lot of things to think about? At first it will seem so, but remember that you do have to make an effort to produce your voice properly and not slip back into old habits. Eventually, with practice, the techniques will become new habits.

—

Stand up and centre yourself.

Read the section again as if to a person across the room. Can you keep your abdominal muscles soft and available for your breath?

Now try the same exercise with a piece of text that you will use or have used in your work.

If you find the breathing difficult, or you are taking bigger breaths than you need, remember the feeling of releasing your throat for those small breaths. You can use that feeling for all your breaths.

Practise it now. Take in quite a quick breath through your mouth as you consciously let your throat relax. You will feel that release mainly at the back of your mouth.

Have a yawn and then try the quick breaths again. Was that easier? Yawning is a great way to release any throat tension or holding.

Now try the reading again.

—

Last-minute checklist

Just before you go into the place where you are to speak – a stage or lecture hall, conference room or classroom – it is useful to have a few things to focus on in order to make sure you are ready to speak well.

Many things might have happened since you warmed up your voice, or since the last time you worked on it: a difficult journey, demanding colleagues or children, pressure of other work or just plain nerves.

So give yourself a moment (it might be in the loo!) to centre yourself, prepare your body and connect to your breath.

> Stand with your feet hip-width apart and be aware of the weight of your feet on the floor. Unlock your knees.
>
> Lift your shoulders up to your ears and then drop them.
>
> Release your abdominal muscles.
>
> Breathe from your abdomen.
>
> Release your neck.
>
> Yawn.
>
> Separate your top teeth from the bottom teeth and let your tongue drop into the bottom of your mouth.
>
> With your teeth apart, silently '**la**' a tune to release your tongue.
>
> Have a drink of water.

If you are in a private place, then add the following:

> Flop over from the waist and let your neck relax. Breathe into your back and abdomen. Roll up slowly.
>
> Hum with your teeth apart, sliding gently down through your range.

Give yourself a moment to be centred. Focus on your low breathing, gather your energy, and you're ready.

CENTRE YOURSELF, STANDING WITH
YOUR FEET HIP-WIDTH APART, YOUR
WEIGHT SPREAD EVENLY ACROSS YOUR
FEET AND YOUR KNEES UNLOCKED.

3.

Voice exercises
– stage 2

VOICE EXERCISES ALWAYS BEGIN WITH BREATHING. IT IS THE MOST IMPORTANT ELEMENT OF GOOD VOICE WORK.

The exercises in Chapter 2 create the foundation for all good voice work. However, when you get to know the work well you might like to move on to the exercises in this chapter. These fall into two categories.

First there are variations on the exercises you have already learnt, giving you new ways to work with your breath and resonance, open sounds and articulation. Then there are exercises for using your voice more powerfully: for calling and shouting, and for finding a very deep support for your voice. These could lead you to experience your breath and voice at a more profound level.

If you have worked thoroughly through the ideas and exercises so far, you should be familiar with the way your body and voice work and be ready to take on new exercises. You might like to build a repertoire of exercises to work from, choosing those that suit the way you feel or your particular needs at any one time.

It is always good to begin your exercises by considering how you are feeling. As with all physical work, you will do it better by first tuning in and focusing on yourself. Then you will be fully aware of how your body is responding.

Breath – finding more breath

Voice exercises always begin with breathing. It is the most important element of good voice work.

Many people like to do their breathing exercises lying on the floor, as it makes them particularly aware of the movement of their abdomen as they breathe. I have given you exercises to try lying on your back, lying face down and kneeling on hands and knees.

You could begin in one position and then change to another as you do your breathing exercises. You could also bring yourself up to standing while doing the exercises.

You might also find that one of these positions is your favourite, or maybe you will like a different position on different days. Some actors use all of them every time they warm up.

Exercise 11: A short cut to low breathing

The position taken in the first part of this exercise, with your knees to the side, can be a shortcut to low abdominal breathing. You don't need to force your breath down as the position of your knees and hips sends the breath there. You will see that it is almost impossible to breathe too high in your chest.

Lie on your back, lift your knees on to your chest and hug them. Breathe down into your abdomen, feeling the movement against your thighs.

Gently lower both knees down to one side of your body (both knees on the same side) and let your arms spread out wide. Stay there as long as you like and enjoy the stretch in your back as your breath is sent down into your abdomen.

Lift your knees up and over to the other side. Try to do this with your abdominal muscles, not using your neck or shoulders. Stay there as long as you like before moving on.

Lift your knees up again on to your abdomen, and then place your feet flat on the floor with your knees pointing up and your feet hip-width apart.

Release at least three long, slow breaths on **S**.
Release at least three long, slow breaths on **Z**.

Count aloud, but not loudly, as far as you can on one breath
without tightening your throat at the end.
Repeat the counting on two more breath releases.

Exercise 12: Breath in your back

The position in this exercise is particularly good for feeling your breath
move into your lower back, at the bottom of your rib cage.

Roll over on to your front and place your forehead on your
hands or arms.
Relax and breathe gently but deeply.
You will gradually feel your lower back engaging with
your breath.
Enjoy the pressure of the floor on your abdomen.
You could do your **S**, **Z** and counting exercises here.

Exercise 13: Releasing your abdominal muscles

In this exercise the position you take allows a very free release of the abdominal muscles. It is good if you know you tend to hold those muscles tightly in everyday life.

––––

Place yourself on your hands and knees.
Enjoy the feeling of your abdomen hanging down, but don't let it draw the middle of your back down with it. The spine should not collapse but remain long.
Breathe deeply.
You could do your **S**, **Z** and counting exercises here.

––––

Exercise 14: Rib work with breath

If you are going to speak loudly for long periods or sing, you need to make full use of your lung capacity. This is a great exercise to stretch your rib cage and feel your lungs fill with air.

——

Stand up, keeping the feeling of your breath coming from your abdomen.
Place your feet hip-width apart.
Make sure there is space between your top and bottom teeth.

Take a big, quick breath in through your mouth, sending it to the sides of your ribs and hold it there for a moment. Then let it go.
Repeat twice more.

——

Breathe through your mouth
Breathe in through your mouth for voice exercises. When we speak, we naturally breathe in through the mouth as it draws air in quickly and easily.

Exercise 15: Rib work with counting

This exercises the lungs, ribs and articulators (jaw, lips and tongue). It also helps to release vocal energy.

——

Use the breathing-in technique of Exercise 14.
Instead of just letting the air go, count aloud repeatedly from one to ten very fast until you run out of air, but not to the point of tightening your throat.

Use lots of face and mouth work as you count.
Repeat twice more.

———

Summary

Experiment with different positions to do your breathing exercises:
— Lie on your back with your knees to one side as a shortcut
  to low breath.
— Lie on your front to focus on breathing into your lower back.
— Hands and knees position will allow you extra abdominal
  release.
— Breathing exercises with rib stretch will extend your lung
  capacity further.

Resonance – from humming to speaking

Start sound smoothly

Whenever you start a sound it is important that it doesn't begin with stickiness or a bang in the throat. We call this 'hard attack' and it is problematic in two ways. First, it can cause damage to the vocal folds if it is very hard and habitual. Second, it wastes breath as the sound bursts out. Your aim is always to feel the sound flow smoothly and easily through your throat from the moment it begins.

Try it now. Make a **Z** and see if you feel the resonance begin immediately in your throat. Although you will feel the buzz on the tip of your tongue, you should also feel vibrations in your throat at the same time, almost as if you were saying a gentle **UZ**. Try a few of those.

Then try a short **Ah**. That may be more difficult to do smoothly. If it is, try a tiny **H** before it: **Hah**.

Every time you make sound in these exercises, try to make the beginning (the 'onset') of sound smooth and resonant.

The next three exercises focus on the space in your throat and awaken the sense of your voice resonating there.

Exercise 16: Throat resonance – single notes

Begin with a yawn or stifled yawn (see the section 'Opening the voice' in Chapter 2) to stretch your throat.

――

Separate your top teeth from your bottom teeth with your lips together. Be aware that there is a space in your throat.

Hum gently into the throat space on a comfortable note. When you feel the resonance is free and full, change note. Try this on several different notes.

――

Exercise 17: Throat resonance – slides

Slide the hum down through your voice, starting with your high, child's voice.
Be aware of the sound travelling through the throat space.
Repeat several times.

Slide the hum around your range.

Exercise 18: Throat resonance – speech

Simply count aloud or speak some words, feeling the resonance in your throat, especially in the vowels.
Some vowels may be less resonant than others. If so, check your tongue-work as you speak them. Can you free it up?

Exercise 19: Using the floor for resonance

Do you remember Exercise 3 where we first tried out resonance? In that exercise you explored feeling the 'buzz' or resonance of your voice in different parts of your body. You released the feeling of the resonance with banging and shaking. In this exercise and Exercise 20 you are going to use gravity to help the resonant voice to move into different areas at the front of your body.

Lie face down on the floor, with your forehead on your hands or arms.

Hum gently on a comfortable note.
Focus that note and then others into your face.
Focus some notes into your chest.

Focus some notes into your abdomen.
Let gravity help you to release the sounds, and resist
any desire to push your voice forward.

Exercise 20: Coming up from the floor

Continue with Exercise 19 and gradually come up on to your
hands and knees.

Move your back around as you hum to feel your voice right
through your body.

Continue with the exercise and come up to standing.
Try to get a sense of bringing the resonance off the floor and
out into the space ahead.

Exercise 21: Resonant words throughout
the body – giving colour to your voice

If you've been practising the resonance exercises regularly, you will
be familiar with thinking your voice into different parts of your body.
You should be feeling and hearing how paying attention to specific
areas of resonance has affected the whole voice, giving more range
and depth to the sound.

Now we are going to try speaking into different parts of the body
to bring all that resonance and range into words. This exercise and
Exercise 22 will particularly help you if you think your voice is rather
flat or monotonous.

Count to ten aloud and focus the resonance into your forehead.

Count to ten aloud and focus the resonance into your nose.

Repeat, focusing the resonance into your lips.

Repeat, focusing the resonance into your chest.

Repeat, focusing the resonance into your abdomen.

Repeat, focusing the resonance on to the top of your head.

Repeat and try to feel the resonance in all the areas at once. You should now feel that your voice is fuller and more colourful.

——

Exercise 22: Sing-song – finding expression and range in speech

——

Count to ten in a 'sing-song' way, swooping and sliding around all the notes of your voice. Use your whole range: high, middle and low notes. At the same time, imagine the resonance of your voice moving all around your body.

Then count to ten normally and you will feel that you have more range in your voice. It will sound more interesting and expressive.

——

Summary

— Throat resonance exercises enhance the sense of voice production without effort.
— You can use the floor as a resonator to help with the free release of a resonant voice.
— Find the colour of your voice by thinking speech into different resonating areas of your body.
— Practise in a 'sing-song' voice to develop expression in speech.

Opening the voice – having fun with shaking and intoning

Sometimes people feel shy of the power of their free voice, so opening it up can be quite scary. The next exercise is to help you to get over this by simply shaking the sound out of you. Enjoy it; it's fun!

Exercise 23: Shaking out sound

——

Breathe down into your abdomen and release a long **Ha** slide down from your high child's voice to the bottom of your voice.

Repeat, but shake your body as you slide your voice. Don't try to keep your voice steady; it will shake too.
Repeat a few more times.

Then repeat the slide without the shaking. Can you retain the feeling of openness and freedom that was there in the shaken voice?

——

Exercise 24: Sustained sound – sending your voice away from you

See if you can now use your free voice on more sustained sounds in this exercise.

——

Breathe down into your abdomen and release a long, sustained **Ha** on any comfortable single note.
Imagine the sound travelling up from the bottom of your abdomen and feel it passing through the throat space.

Repeat on different notes.
Try to think of the sound of your voice going away from you.

It's a good idea to look at something across the room and send your voice to that place. Be sure that the energy of your voice doesn't dip or drop as you finish the sound. Keep the sense of voice from your abdomen throughout. Then you will be supporting it with your breath.

───

Intoning

The next three exercises use intoning, which is a very useful way to open up the voice. Intoning is simply speaking on one steady note without the usual rise and fall of normal speech. Think of it as half singing, half speaking. Like singing, it allows you to enjoy the feeling of the resonance of your voice being released into words, but without the worry of getting the tune right. Because it is sustained like singing, it also demands that you use good breath support from your abdomen.

Intoning is a way to experience and develop the free power of your voice. But it can also reveal your speech habits. People often feel rather exposed when they first try intoning, especially if they are not used to singing. In normal speech we have control over the way we deliver words. We control speed, volume and intonation patterns. We strengthen or reduce the energy and length of vowels and consonants. These are then integrated with physical expression. Some of this control can be unhelpful, leading to tightening of the jaw, throat or shoulders.

Intoning wipes all those controls away and should be a pure release of the voice – a voice that responds easily to your thinking. However, the purity of the sound can connect very deeply to emotion and make you feel vulnerable, especially if you are working with other people.

You have to be brave as you first try the exercises. If you find that your jaw, throat or shoulders tighten and restrict the free release of sound, give your body a little shake out. Connect to your deep breath support by flopping over from the waist or squatting down. Then stand up again, centre yourself and take the exercises slowly. In order to get the best experience of intoning, you have to let go of tension in your speech and breathing mechanisms. Try to resist pushing the sound out. It doesn't have to be loud but shouldn't be too quiet either: just an easy release of sustained sound.

Exercises 25: Intoned words

The aim of this exercise is to experience open, intoned speech being released into the room and reaching across the space.

———

Check your posture, low breath and space between your teeth.

On a comfortable note, intone counting to ten.
Think the sound away from you across the room.

Change the note and repeat.
Do this several times on different notes.

———

You must make sure you start each word exactly on the note, rather than lurching up to it. If this happens, you are probably tightening your throat. Your voice should flow through the words.

Now try intoning some speech. It could be a speech from a play, or perhaps something you have written yourself or need to read for your work. Why not find a poem you like? Alternatively, you could count or use the days of the week or months of the year.

If you are reading your piece, try to organise it a bit at a time so that you don't look down at the page until you have finished a phrase or line of text. You should try to 'see' it land across the room before you look at the next bit.

For example, you could organise the beginning of *Pride and Prejudice* like this:

It is a truth universally acknowledged,

that a single man in possession of a good fortune,

must be in want of a wife.

However little known the feelings or views of such a man may be

on his first entering a neighbourhood,

this truth is so well fixed in the minds of the surrounding families,

that he is considered as the rightful property

of some one or other of their daughters.

— Jane Austen

Enjoy the feeling of the sound of your voice flowing through the words. Breathe in whenever you need to.

Exercise 26: Intoning into speaking

———

Intone counting to ten again on one comfortable note.

Take a breath and immediately repeat the counting but this time in normal speech. Try to allow the same sense of releasing the sound forward across the room as you did when intoning.

Repeat several times from a different intoned note each time; intone, breath, speak,
intone, breath, speak.

Now try this with your speech or piece of text. Intone a section, breathe, then speak that section.
Repeat this throughout the entire text, then speak the whole piece normally.

———

The idea is to retain the feeling of your voice flowing away from you through the words, even though you are now speaking with normal intonation. It shouldn't sound unnatural: just free and open.

Exercise 27: Intoning and shaking into speech

——

Repeat Exercise 26 but this time shake your body as you
intone. Then be still again for speaking. This should help to free
up your voice and make it sound as if it is coming from your
whole body.

Finally, speak the piece again in normal speech, remembering
the freedom of intoning and shaking.

——

Summary

Don't be afraid of the power of your voice. Enjoy it. Release its
power with:
— shaking
— sustained vowels
— intoning.

Articulation – tongue twisters

Exercise 28: Tongue twisters

I expect you remember trying tongue twisters when you were a child. They are a brilliant way to get the speech muscles moving and dexterous. Your aim with them now is not to wow your friends with your speed, or give up if you can't do them easily. It is to practise them until you are accurate and clear with all the consonants.

Begin by doing them carefully and precisely, making sure you are aware of all the various tongue movements needed to achieve the right sounds. Notice if there are consonants that you habitually miss out or pronounce too softly – perhaps a T or an L at the end of a word. Then gradually speed up, repeating each sentence over and over without missing any consonants.

It can be very useful to practise them silently first; mouthing them and moving the mouth and tongue a little more than normal. This gives you a chance to really feel where the tongue should go. Then speak them aloud. Gradually go faster and faster – but always accurately.

Big, bad, bold, brilliant Brown
Bewildered in Wimbledon
A pretty, pink petticoat
A practical proposition to propagate the appetite
Many merry mandolins
An incredibly incongruous incriminating cryptogram
Down in the Delta doing dreadful deeds deliberately
Dan drank the drink and got drunk
Ten tonnes of tarmac tumbled out of the truck
Tick tock, tick tack, tick tock, tick tack
They were fearful for the health of the philosopher Thrasea
Feel the voice flow freely through the throat
Seventy-seven sailors standing sentry on the strand
They strung a strong string straight across the street
Rhetorical philanthropists are generally lugubrious
A lucky, little stickleback

Using your voice powerfully

Strong support of your voice

If you have to speak loudly for sustained periods, or need to shout or call out, your voice needs to be strongly supported from the muscles deep within your body. If it is not, there is a danger of losing your voice or causing it harm.

On the stages of the National Theatre the actors always try to speak with well-supported voices.

In everyday life, if you need your voice to act powerfully in a particular situation, it usually does so naturally and effectively, because the need stimulates the action. Think of screaming in fright or yelling in anger. It gets the attention you want, but it is unlikely to hurt your voice because your brain sends the right messages to your breath and muscles to get the job done.

If we recreate these situations, we can learn how our body reacts spontaneously. Then we can use our muscle memory to engage a strong support of the voice in less spontaneous situations.

Let's try some of these.

Exercise 29: Calling out

Imagine you want to call to your mum when she is in another room. Can you picture it? Now try it. **Mum! Mum!**
Did you feel your abdominal muscles engage?

Try it again quite loudly.

What if someone was about to run across a road in front of a bus? You'd shout, **Stop! Stop!**
Try it. Did you feel those muscles engage?

What about a football chant? **United! United!** (or whatever your club is).

What you are probably feeling is a slight tightening in the area around your diaphragm and also some sensation lower down, near your groin, as the muscles of support kick into action. You'll be experiencing these sensations at the top and the bottom of your abdomen.

To use these muscles to support a loud or sustained voice, you must not try to push or pump with them. Instead, allow them to work by first breathing down to them and then placing the energy of your voice there.

If this seems a little abstract, try this more physical exercise.

Exercise 30: Hand pressing for support

––––

Press the heels of your hands together in front of you, just at the height of your diaphragm.
Breathe. You may feel your breath drawn in very deeply and your rib cage widen.
Take some time with this to allow your body and thoughts to come together.

Try Exercise 29 again with the hands pressed together. Did you feel your breath drop low in your body? Did your voice feel supported and strong, coming from deep in your body?
Try it again – you could do it a few times.

Now try it without pressing your hands together and see if your muscle memory allows the same support and strength.

Try counting fairly loudly from this place.

Try the speech or piece of work you used in Exercise 25, and speak it loudly enough to fill a large room or theatre.
You could use the hand pressing at any time to feel the deep support engage.

––––

Although I am suggesting hand pressing here to help you when you need to use your voice powerfully, you will find that it helps any kind

of voice use. Many people find it a quick and efficient way to support the breath and voice. Some actors use it just before they go on stage. You could add it to your last-minute checklist.

Along with the deep support muscles coming into action when you call out spontaneously, your body also takes in enough breath to make the right sound. To recreate this, you must take in enough breath and breathe frequently. Allow the thought of what you are going to call out to stimulate the in-breath.

> **Don't forget to breathe!**
> That probably sounds obvious but I say it to actors of all ages and levels of experience more than anything else. If you don't breathe often enough and deeply enough, you and your listeners will get tired.

Calling and shouting

The next two exercises take the strong support work from calling to shouting. For these techniques it is important that you don't lower the pitch of your voice. If you think back to Exercise 29 where we were using examples of strong support from real life, when you called out **Mum!** or **Stop!** you probably pitched your voice up a bit. Your brain knows instinctively that high sounds travel quicker.

Remind yourself of that by calling out **Hey!** as if to someone in the distance. Did you hear that? To recreate this, it can be useful to think your voice up and over the space.

Exercise 31: Extending the call

———

Check your posture, breath and space between your teeth.
Use the hand pressing from Exercise 30 if you wish.
Breathe in through your mouth and call out **One** from deep

support, letting your voice find a pitch a bit higher than
normal speech.
Breathe in through the mouth and call **One, Two** in the
same way.
Breathe in and call **One**, **Two**, **Three**.
Breathe in and call **One**, **Two**, **Three**, **Four**.
Continue counting in the same way until you have reached
the limit of your breath support without tightening your throat.

————

As you get towards the end of your support, you will probably feel your
muscles engaging more and more. You will also feel the increased
need for breath. Enjoy those feelings and lock them in your memory.

Exercise 32: Shouting

To take this strong support work into shouting, you need to use much
more movement in your face and articulators. When a person really
shouts, their face screws up and their lips protrude. These actions help
to send the voice forward out of the body, the lips acting like the horn
of a trumpet. Thinking the voice out through the bridge of the nose is
also helpful, as it directs the energy of the voice away from the throat.

You also need to use the consonants firmly, as a springboard into the
vowels. In general, we feel that vowels carry emotion, but consonants,
especially those at the beginning of words or syllables, provide the
muscularity that releases the vowels.

————

Check your posture, breath and the space between your
teeth again.
Try this exercise with and without hand pressing (see
Exercise 30).

Breathe in through your mouth and shout out **No!** from deep
support, letting your voice find a pitch a bit higher than
normal speech.

Breathe in through your mouth and shout out **No don't!** in the same way.

Breathe in and shout out **No don't go!**

Feel how the muscularity of the **N**, the **D** and the **G** sounds helps you to release the emotion in the vowel safely.

Try not to let your jaw tighten or clamp shut, as this will stop the true, free sound from coming out and you might hurt your throat.

Make sure that the last word you say is as supported and as loud as the first. It is very common for people to lose confidence and support at the end of a phrase.

Finish the exercise by sliding down though your voice on a hum a couple of times. This is like a little vocal-fold massage, which soothes the muscles after the shock of shouting.

———

Exercise 33: Checking your abdomen

If you feel that you are straining or pushing from your throat, it can be useful to do the exercises on hands and knees.

———

Go down on to your hands and knees, making sure your back is long and not collapsed in the middle.

Allow your weight to be supported on the heels of your hands. Feel how relaxed your abdomen is.

Repeat Exercises 31 and 32 in this position, or try any speech or words and phrases you need to shout or call out for your work.

Can you feel your abdomen's automatic response to the energy of your voice?

You will also feel your voice easily falling forward into your face, and your jaw and mouth will feel very mobile.

ENJOY SPEAKING LOUDLY, CLEARLY, FULLY, EXPRESSIVELY AND EASILY.

Stand up and repeat the exercises, being sure to keep your abdomen soft to allow it to respond naturally.

———

By now you should be able to feel how the freedom of your abdomen allows your breath to support the sound without tightening your throat.

Exercise 34: Working on a text with volume and strong support

It is now time to bring the work together on a piece of text: a speech from a play, a poem or perhaps a report you have to present at a meeting. Work from good, deep support, with open resonance, clear articulation and at a louder volume than you use in normal conversation. Actors could choose a passionate or emotional piece of text. It could be a text you already know.

The volume you choose is up to you, depending on where you are likely to have to speak. If you are an actor, have an idea of a big theatre; if you are a teacher or a minister of religion, imagine a large classroom or place of worship. Even if you only have to speak at a meeting in a conference room, you should probably be speaking louder than normal. I often attend meetings where I can't hear speakers across a table that is only a little bigger than an average dining table.

Why not try the work outside? This can be useful as there are likely to be fewer hard surfaces for your voice to bounce off. This means that your technique will have to be precise.

It is always helpful to have someone you trust to hear you and respond honestly to what you are doing.

———

Check that your knees are not locked and that your weight is balanced in the centre of your feet.
Release your shoulders.
Release the spaces in your mouth and throat.

Take the piece slowly, being aware of how the ideas or thoughts are structured.

Look out into the distance of your space, ready to let your voice reach across it.

Allow time for the breath to drop in, stimulated by thought. Speak from deep support in your abdomen.

Enjoy the resonance of your voice in your mouth, throat and, with practice, in the rest of your body.

Allow your jaw to be free enough to move easily, and feel the energetic movement of your articulators.

Be sure to support your voice to the very end of each phrase, and don't allow the volume to fade away. The last words of a thought are often the most important.

———

Enjoy speaking loudly, clearly, fully, expressively and easily.

Summary

— The body and voice work together naturally when you feel a real need to shout or call out. Use the memory of these real-life experiences in your voice and body when you are calling and shouting words and phrases.
— Don't forget to breathe!
— Use hand pressing to experience deep support in your abdomen. If you are tightening your abdominal muscles, try the exercises on hands and knees.

4.

Preparing your voice for performance

THIS SORT OF VOICE USE IS ATHLETIC,
AND NO ATHLETE WOULD DREAM OF
EXERCISING WITHOUT WARMING UP.

Warming up your voice for performance is an extremely important part of best practice and vocal health. Like an athlete, you need to prepare your breathing muscles and the muscles of your vocal tract for an extended or strenuous performance. A play or musical certainly requires you to warm up your voice first. But other situations may also demand this, especially if you have to work at some volume. A sermon, lecture or presentation, or even a day in the classroom, may all need a warm-up first.

This chapter brings together some of the exercises you have already learnt in a structured way that will prepare you for your work. It is the warm-up I give to actors at the National Theatre. Once you know the routine, you can give it as much or as little time as you wish, depending on the needs of your work. As little as ten minutes would make a big difference to your voice production.

After strenuous or continued voice use, laryngologists recommend that you also warm down your voice. The idea behind the warm-down exercises in this chapter is to release any physical tensions that may have developed during the performance and re-establish good muscle action in the vocal folds throughout the range. Warming down also contributes to your preparation for your next performance.

Good voice use is intended not just for the duration of your performance. How you use your voice in the rest of your life is just as important, and will have a strong effect on the times you are required to use it strenuously (professional voice users should be careful when talking in noisy places like pubs and clubs, or some restaurants).

If your performance has been vocally demanding and you don't warm down, the muscles that produce your voice will continue to carry the effects of this. Think again of the athlete who always stretches and releases after their sport as well as before.

Warming up

To prepare, first stretch out your upper body. You can do this in any way you like, but you could use the stretches from Chapter 2.

Breath

Centre yourself, standing with your feet hip-width apart, your weight spread evenly across your feet, and your knees unlocked. Become aware of your whole body and then notice your breath.

Flop over from the waist and breathe into your lower back and abdomen.

Squat to feel your breath deep in your lower body.

Squatting, standing or lying on your back (knees to the side first, if you wish), massage your jaw muscles, face and neck.

Release at least three breaths on a long, slow S.
Release at least three breaths on a long, slow Z.
Release at least three long breaths, counting aloud as far as you can without straining.

Resonance

Hum into your face, throat, chest, abdomen and back. You can do this in any position that helps you to avoid pushing your voice: lying down, kneeling, on all fours, standing or sitting.
You could use your hands to pat, bang or massage your body.

Hum gently and high into the top of your head.

Stand up and centre yourself.

Slide a hum down from top to bottom a few times – think the sound up and out.

Opening the voice

Rib stretches
Stretch over to the side with your arm over your head, as you learnt in Chapter 1. Breathe into the stretched side of your ribs.

Drop the elbow and shoulder forward to breathe into the back of the ribs.

Repeat on the other side.

Yawn and stifled yawn
Do the yawn or stifled yawn to stretch your throat.

Open sounds
Slide down through the range of your voice on **Ha** a few times, sending the sound up and out.

Slide down on other vowels.

Intoning
Release long, intoned vowels on any notes you like across the space.
Take one vowel per breath and use your deep breath support. Change the note for each new breath.

Intone counting or some text on one note, with the same sense of releasing sounds across the space. Use your breath support.

Repeat, speaking normally, with the same sense of releasing your voice across the space and the same breath support.
You could use hand pressing for open sounds and intoning, to increase your sense of support.

Articulation and words

Use any repeated consonants and vowels, exercising the tip of your tongue, the back of your tongue and your lips.

Try some tongue twisters.

Text
Speak any text you like, mouthing the words without any voice. This will help you to feel the shapes of the words in your mouth.

Then whisper the text, being careful not to push the sounds in your throat. This will make you aware of the energy of the consonants as you feel your breath passing through them.

Then speak the text quietly but with good support, keeping the sound forward and out. This will help you to feel the resonance of your voice.

Finally, speak the text at the right volume for the space you are going to work in.

Warming down

Body tension release
Flop over from the waist and bounce or shake out your body. You could allow your voice to sound at the same time.
Hang still and breathe into your abdomen and lower back.

Roll up through your spine until you are standing tall and centred, with your breath low.

Lift your shoulders up to your ears without moving your head. Then let them drop back into place.
Repeat if you wish.

Use a yawn or stifled yawn to release any throat and jaw tension.

Voice release
Heavy voice use may put stress on one particular part of the vocal folds, depending on the pitch used. The next exercise helps to release that stress.

In this exercise you are engaging breath support throughout your range, from high pitch to low. In high pitch, the vocal folds stretch and the vibrations are faster than in lower pitches. So sliding down the range is a releasing action.

Taking breath from your abdomen, slide a hum down through your range from top to bottom.
Repeat several times.
Take the high note from your gentle, child's voice above the pitch break. Try not to strain for it. Think it there.

Hydration
Sip some water at room temperature (not iced).

Steaming is a very good way to stay hydrated or re-establish hydration. You could simply use a bowl of water with a towel over your head, or buy a cosmetic or medical steamer.
Use only water, without anything added.

If you are in a play and you have a scene where you have to shout or scream, you should always slide down on a hum a few times when you come off stage.

Then you should warm down thoroughly at the end of the play.

STEAMING IS A GOOD WAY TO STAY
HYDRATED OR RE-ESTABLISH HYDRATION.

5.

Applying the exercises to your voice problems

SUPPORT YOUR VOICE PROPERLY
WITH YOUR BREATHING, AS BREATH
IS THE ENERGY OF THE VOICE.

Throughout this book I have told you that you will achieve the best, longest-lasting improvement in the way you speak if you establish a strong foundation by working with all the sections in Chapters 2 and 3: breath, resonance, opening the voice and articulation. This will teach you the proper way to use your voice for life. However, you may also like to know which of the exercises will help you to address particular voice or speech problems that you are concerned about.

Here are suggestions for problems that I often come across. Although I include specific exercises for particular issues, I must stress that everything begins with correct breathing and release of physical tensions.

Audibility

If you mumble

Work on opening your mouth more by loosening up the back of your jaw. The joint of your upper and lower jaw is in front of your ear on each side of your face. There is a muscle that joins the two jaws together and it can easily get tight, especially when you are nervous. Massaging this muscle helps to release it. Place your fingertips in front of your ear lobe on each side and massage that area. If you are not sure you are at the right place, bite your teeth together and you will feel the muscle knot up on the bottom jaw. Release the bite and massage that area.

If the mouth is held quite closed, the tongue can't work freely enough for clarity. Then the sound of your voice is unable to come through properly. Try to establish a new habit of carrying your jaw with space between your teeth, even when your mouth is closed.

Then read something aloud to practise speaking with the back of your jaw released. At first you may feel that your mouth is too open and that you have to move your lips too much. Why not take a look at yourself in a mirror as you speak with the released jaw? You'll be

surprised at how normal you look. When your mouth was held quite closed you probably weren't moving your lips enough for your words to be clear.

Exercises 1, 2, 5 and 8 – and practise the tongue twisters (Exercise 28).

If your voice is too quiet

Support your voice properly with your breathing, as breath is the energy of the voice. You also need to make sure that you are using your mouth effectively for speech sounds to shape the energy of the words you use. Work particularly on discovering the resonance of your voice (Exercises 3, 4 and 5). You may have to be brave about using your voice more loudly. Check in a mirror to see that using more energy for articulation doesn't look exaggerated.

Exercises 1 to 9.

Breath control

If you get short of breath

Try all the breathing exercises, but especially Exercises 1 and 2, and the deep support exercises (Exercises 29 to 33). Take particular note of the use of the low ribs in the sections 'Preparation – stretches, posture and abdominal release' and 'Breath – breathing deeply to support your voice'.

If your voice is too breathy

Make sure you are using the resonance of your voice properly, allowing it out with good breath support through a relaxed throat. The voice can sound breathy if you are using the muscles of your throat to control your voice. This habit tightens your throat and interferes with the action of your vocal folds.

Work with the all the resonance exercises (Exercises 3 and 4, and 16 to 22), but make sure you have done some breathing exercises first.

Vocal stamina

If your voice gets tired easily

Your voice will tire if you aren't breathing freely and deeply enough, and supporting your voice with your breath. Any unnecessary tension in your throat or jaw will also tire your voice.

Exercises 1 to 5.

If your throat sometimes aches or feels scratchy

When you speak for long periods, especially if you are speaking loudly, you will be working the muscles of your throat quite hard. As with any form of prolonged physical exercise, the muscles may start to feel tired or achy. However, if you have a scratchy feeling inside your throat then you are not using a properly supported voice, with easy access to breath. This means your throat has to work too hard to create the voice you want.

Keep practising the exercises in Chapter 2 to learn how to breathe deeply into your body and support your voice from your abdomen.

Try yawning or using the stifled yawn (see the section 'Opening the voice' in Chapter 2) to find immediate release of throat tension. You could also shrug your shoulders to release tension there. Then practise Exercise 30: Hand pressing for support. You can use this technique as a way to engage your deep support for any type of speaking, not just for a powerful voice.

EVERYTHING BEGINS WITH
CORRECT BREATHING AND
RELEASE OF PHYSICAL TENSIONS.

Keep them listening

If you need more authority in your voice

Knowing how to use your voice properly will allow you to use it with authority whenever you wish to. However, while you are still learning the techniques, there are three things you could focus on when you want to show you mean business:

> **Engage deep support for your voice.** Have another look at the section 'Supporting your voice' in Chapter 2 and the section 'Strong support of your voice' in Chapter 3. These exercises are not just for speaking loudly. They will help you whenever you need to be firm and authoritative, even with a quiet voice.

> **Carry your voice through to the ends of your thoughts** without getting quiet or breathy on the last word or words. This will sustain your commitment to what you are saying.

> **Use firm consonants**, especially at the beginnings of words. Practise the tongue twisters (Exercise 28) using lots of muscular energy in your mouth and tongue.

Finally, a strong sense of your feet making contact with the ground will help you to feel strong and rooted, both physically and vocally. But be sure you don't lock your knees back. If you lock the knees you will lock the breath.

If you want your voice to be more interesting

To keep people's attention, you need to have a voice that moves easily over your whole range in a natural way. Working with the resonance exercises throughout your range will help you to achieve this.

Exercises 3, 5, 21 and 22.

Summary

— Ask yourself which vocal habits you need to correct. Someone else might help you to identify what is stopping you from using your voice well.
— Make sure you practise correct breathing and release of throat tension before you start the specific exercises for your problem.

6.

Speaking clearly in your own accent

AUTHENTICITY OF SPEECH
IS TO BE DESIRED AND ALL
ACCENTS CAN BE CLEAR.

'Estuary English'

Many modern British accents have developed common features around the loss or mispronunciation of certain consonants. It has been suggested that this is the result of the influence of London sounds on accents from other areas of the country. These sounds have been spread through the media – you can hear them in the voices of many British celebrities now.

David Rosewarne in the *Times Educational Supplement* (19 October 1984) drew attention to the London influence on Standard English or Received Pronunciation (RP) and coined the phrase 'Estuary English'. He predicted that London sounds would eventually be heard all over the country. Today, not everyone would agree that their regional accent is affected by London sounds. However, television, radio and the internet have become a powerful part of our culture, and strongly influence trends in vocabulary and pronunciation.

If you are not British, you may find that something similar is happening to your own country's sounds.

All accents can be clear

I must make it clear that I don't disapprove of Estuary English or any other accent, nor am I advocating Standard English (or Standard American, or any other 'standard') as a required accent for clear speech. Authenticity of speech is to be desired (see the section 'Who you are' in Chapter 1), and all accents can be clear. But a regional accent that retains all of its strongest features at all times can exclude listeners who are not from that region.

In theatre training, actors not only learn to speak in accents other than their own; they also learn to use their native accent with clarity and muscularity, in a manner that opens up their particular world to audiences.

Overcoming consonant weaknesses

The following exercises focus on consonant weaknesses found in many modern British accents. These problem sounds can be overcome, although in my experience it takes some time and work. The exercises consist of short passages that repeatedly use a problem sound. Read them aloud and practise until the problem sound is easily pronounced.

L at the ends of words and before consonants often disappears or sounds like W

Practise making an **L**. Do you feel where the tip of your tongue hits the roof of your mouth, close to your front teeth? You must make sure you feel that every time you make an **L**. Try not to round your lips at the same time, unless there is an **O** before the **L**.

Now read aloud:

The old man was full of a cold. He told the children he'd be beholden to them if only they'd hold off their yells until he'd boiled the kettle to fill his hot water bottle.
'I hope I don't have to go to hospital,' he grumbled.
His sister Mildred made him some scrambled eggs and hot milk, and he took some garlic oil capsules that he held to be of special help.

He was the uncle of Bill Holt, a minister who had built up quite a cult following in Wimbledon, where his heartfelt moral discourses from the pulpit had received tumultuous applause from evangelicals. However, Bill's hold on his fold altered when an occult cell unfurled a childish banner in the chapel, and a girl hurled abuse at the whole caboodle. The culprits were later caught in a field and handled coldly by churlish church officials before being bundled away by railway.

A weak R

To make a clear **R**, your lips must come forward to allow your tongue to make the right shape. This usually happens just before the **R**. Try it, and you should also feel the sides of your tongue come up to the inside of your teeth ridge for support. If you can feel the tip of your tongue, it should be pointing up towards your palette.

Now read aloud:

Little Red Riding Hood wasn't frightened in the forest. She ran rapidly through it to her grandmother's house and rapped on the door. When her grandmother answered, her voice sounded rough and strange, but Red Riding Hood readily released the latch and pranced into the room. Her old grandmother was reclining in bed so she took her basket of red apples over to her.

'Oh Grandmamma,' she said, 'your eyes are enormous. Have you been reading too much?'

'No,' cried Grandmamma, 'I want to have a really good look at my granddaughter.'

'Oh Grandmamma, are you wearing great big gloves? Your hands are very hairy.'

'No deary, I've been scrubbing the range and they've grown rough and raw.'

'Oh Grandmamma, your teeth are ridiculously big and razor sharp. Right, I'm off. Something's very wrong here.'

Little Red Riding Hood ran from the house, straight through the forest and reached her home in record time. When her mother asked why she was so out of breath, Little Red Riding Hood tried to tell her the truth. But her mother said, 'Rubbish! You probably ate the red apples then fell asleep and dreamed it all. You can go right back and tell Grandmother how sorry you are.'

Red Riding Hood did as she was told and the rest is history.

DO YOU MISS OUT OR MISPRONOUNCE ANY CONSONANTS? HOW ABOUT NG, L, R, S, T, TH?

S often slides back to SH when followed by other consonants, especially TR

Practise the difference between **S** and **SH**. For **S**, the tip of your tongue is very close to the roof of your mouth, near your top teeth. For **SH**, you will feel a bit of pressure in the sides of your tongue. Go quickly from one to the other: **S–SH, S–SH, S–SH, S–SH**.

Then quite slowly practise sliding from **S** to **TR**. Do you feel the action of the three different consonants? It feels like a little lick, doesn't it? But there should be no hint of **SH**. Your lips should come forward as you move into the **R** to give room for the tongue to make the proper shape.

Now read aloud:

> Brian Brown straightened his striped tie and ran his strong hands through his streaked hair.
>
> The strap of the strongbox snapped and struck the stranger's outstretched arm.
>
> The strain of struggling with the Stradivarius caused the student much stress.
>
> A stranger tried to strangle Struan but Struan outstripped him and threw him into a stream.
>
> School felt like a straightjacket to Stephen.
>
> Some straggling strawberries grew over the strange structure.
>
> The strategy is strict but straightforward.

T at the end of a word is often missed in connected speech, which can be perfectly acceptable but not if it causes a lack of clarity

T is most commonly missed when it comes before a vowel, either in the middle of a word or between words. Try saying, 'That apple, but I, what if, later on, better, hotter, daughter, wanted'. Make sure the tip of your tongue taps your palette for every **T**.

Now read aloud:

> It was late afternoon when Pete went out into the garden. It
> was still hot and humid, so he sat in the shade under a tree,
> but even there he was sweating. He was waiting to meet an
> aunt of his wife, who might offer him a job in her bottling plant.
> His mate Andy shouted from inside the house, 'What are you
> going to do tonight if that old woman doesn't appear?'
> 'I don't know,' he replied, 'I suppose I'll get over it and go out
> for a pint of beer. How about you, what are you doing later?'
> 'Oh I've got a date at eight with a beautiful girl called Kate, so
> don't expect to see me till late.'
> A bit later on when the aunt arrived she found Pete fast
> asleep on the grass with a half-drunk pint of bitter at his elbow.
> 'So you started a bit early, didn't you?' she said, as she nudged
> him with her toe. 'You might have waited for me. I've got a bit
> of a thirst on me what with all this heat. And anyway, I like a
> pint at this time of night. It helps me to sleep. So do you want
> the job or not?'

TH pronounced as F, especially with an F nearby

Practise the difference between **F** and **TH**. For **F**, your top teeth touch
your bottom lip. For **TH**, the tip of your tongue almost touches the
back of your top teeth. You can make **TH** in two different ways: one
is all breath and the other is vibration. The breath **TH** is in the words
'theatre', 'through', 'thief', 'wealth'. The vibrating **TH** is in the words
'this', 'then', 'feather', 'breathe'. Go quickly from one to the other: **TH–F,
TH–F, TH–F, TH–F**. Try both the breath one and the vibrating one.

Now read aloud:

> This is Keith the thief and his brother Fred with the filthy teeth.
> Their father had taught them to be thrifty, so at his death Fred
> thought he'd save the money he'd been bequeathed by hiding
> it underneath the turf in a weather-beaten spot on the heath.

Keith the thief was thirsty for wealth. So he followed his brother stealthily to the heath and watched him thrust the money into the turf. It lay beneath a cliff, which was three thousand feet high, with a path forged into the cliff face.

As Keith fought through the ferns that thronged around the foot of the cliff, Fred heard his footsteps and thrust his fist into the thicket. His fist came in contact with his brother's face, forcing Keith to think whether it was worth it to fight Fred and filch the wealth, or to flit fast with a throbbing face.

ING sometimes loses its G, being spoken as just IN

To make an **ING**, the back of your tongue lifts up to the back of the roof of your mouth. Practise a series of them: **ING, ING, ING, ING**.

Now read aloud:

If you are thinking of taking singing lessons to further your career, you should be prepared to work on your breathing. You may be feeling it high in your chest, and your singing teacher will help you to relax, bringing your breathing down. You shouldn't be tightening your throat but releasing your voice in a smooth, flowing sound. You shouldn't be lifting your shoulders either. Instead, you should be allowing them to hang easily as you sing.

If things go well you could be getting a recording contract very soon with a leading label and making enough money to send you laughing all the way to the bank. So don't go forgetting me giving you this advice for nothing when you're sitting in the lap of luxury. You should be remembering friends on your way up as you may be needing them again on your way down.

TALKIN

G

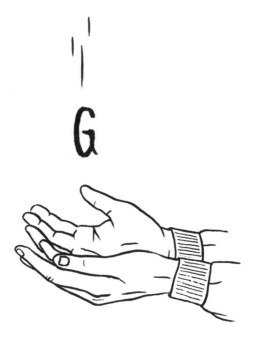

Summary

- You don't have to speak Standard English or Standard American to be clear, but you do need to speak your own accent clearly to people from other regions.
- Ask yourself if you miss out or mispronounce any consonants: **NG, L, R, S, T, TH**. Which do you need to correct so you don't exclude your listeners? Regular practice of these exercises will correct any problem sounds.

7.

Communicating with your voice

GOOD VOICE TECHNIQUE LETS
YOUR AUDIENCE LISTEN TO
WHAT IS BEING SAID, NOT TO
WHO SAYS IT OR HOW IT IS SAID.

If you are a teacher, a minister or in business, you know that good verbal communication is vital to your work. However, getting your message across is not just a case of using a clear and healthy voice.

Getting into the listener's ear

In work, on stage and possibly in life, when we open our mouths to speak we are usually trying to persuade somebody of something. To do that effectively, we have to get into the ear of the listener. Unfortunately, there are many things that can get in the way of that seemingly simple act.

When I work away from the theatre with teachers or business people who wish to improve their voice and communication skills, there are certain habits that I see again and again. These habits, which are usually unknown to the speaker, stop ideas, messages and images from reaching the listener's ear and therefore their mind.

Getting to know your bad habits

I would like to share some of these with you so that you can look out for them yourself. You may need some help with this. You could be brave enough to ask a friend to listen to you deliver a speech or watch you teach. Or why not record yourself using voice memo on your phone or, even better, using video?

Sustaining vocal energy and keeping it interesting

Voice dropping away at the end of thoughts

This can happen through the last few words, or on the last word of a thought or sentence. It is important that you become aware of the end of each thought before you move on to the next one. In English, it is quite common for the intonation at the end of a thought to go down. But without changing this or sounding unnatural, you can keep the voice sustained to the end of whatever you are saying.

It can be useful to imagine that you are throwing a ball out into the audience on the last word of your thought or sentence. You need the ball to land with the listeners and you must see it land. So if you are reading, try to keep your eyes up off the page and with the audience on the last word or phrase of the sentence before looking down for the next sentence. This is a technique you need to practise as you may fear you will lose your place at first. But it is easier than you may think. Try it now with any book or text you have to hand.

You need to maintain the sense of connection to your supported voice throughout, and make sure you don't withdraw vocal energy or go into a whisper. The end of your thought or sentence can often be the most important part.

Repeated tunes

This habit is most likely to occur if you are reading your speech. You may be ending each thought or sentence in exactly the same way, or landing on exactly the same note every time. This habit tends to bore the listener and stop them hearing properly. It can also be irritating, as the speaker doesn't seem to be engaged with what they are saying.

To avoid this, think of your speech as a story you are telling or some ideas you are exploring. I don't mean to suggest that you talk to your audience as if they are children. But if you really talk *to* them, not *at* them, you will naturally maintain variety in the music and intonation

TALK TO YOUR LISTENERS, NOT AT THEM.

of your speech. Remember, giving a speech or lecture is not a solo activity. It needs at least two people: a speaker and a listener. Both of them are taking an active part in the process. It might be helpful to remember that you are not on your own out there, and your listeners do want to be engaged by what you are saying. They have come to hear what you have to say.

Regulating pace, volume and speed

Speaking too fast

You have to practise aloud to get the right pace without feeling unnaturally slow. Again, it is helpful to remember that you are talking *to* people, not *at* them, and you want them to follow and think about what you are saying.

Sometimes people go too fast at the beginning of thoughts; racing to get to the first stressed word or main point of a sentence. You need to lead your listeners to the points you are making, not make them run after you.

Also, don't fall into the trap of thinking that your listeners want you to get it over with quickly. This indicates that you are being too self-conscious. It is not you who matters but the content of what you are delivering. Good voice technique allows your audience to listen to what is being said, not who says it or how it is said.

Speaking too quietly

I often hear people giving talks where they seem to be communicating with only the front row. This is partly to do with where you look. You must have a sense of the back row of your audience in order to project your voice and ideas there. You do have to look at the whole audience.

Using good physical habits

Eye contact

Following on from the previous point, eye contact is a very powerful tool. Yes, you must include the whole room in your gaze. But making eye contact briefly with individuals can really draw people to you and what you are saying. This applies to big audiences, smaller groups and even individuals.

However, make sure you don't hold someone's gaze for so long that they feel uncomfortable. It should be just long enough to connect to them. Keeping your eyes up in the room to the end of a thought or sentence will also help you to keep the vocal energy going, and give more weight to the whole thought.

Do you have a 'tell'?

A 'tell' is the word used in poker to describe the small, unconscious movement that gives away a player's bluff. I think most of us have a 'tell' that appears when we are nervous. It would be good for you to find out what yours is. You may have to ask someone who knows you well.

Some of the 'tells' I see are stiffened, clenched or twitchy fingers; tapping feet; bouncing knee (common in men, and usually when sitting); a lifted shoulder; and a tilting head or lifted chin. There are others.

Moving your mouth

Be sure to use your mouth enough when you speak (I don't mean in an exaggerated way!). It is worth checking in a mirror. You may find you move yours much less than you think.

We understand a lot of what people say by watching their lips – and, of course, not everyone listening to you will have the best of hearing.

Standing and sitting well

You need to have your weight evenly balanced across your feet, and your knees unlocked, even if you are standing with your feet together. Do look out for this when wearing heels, as they tend to throw the weight back. When your weight is pulled back on to your heels, your voice is also pulled back and you will find speaking freely much more difficult.

This balanced, upright posture, without strain, will also help you to appear confident, and will draw your listeners to you. If you pull your weight back or slump down it will seem as if you lack confidence in your message.

If you are sitting down to speak, it is a good idea to have at least one of your feet flat on the ground. Try it, then try with both feet tilted away from the ground. It feels different, doesn't it? One or both feet flat on the ground helps to root you and allows better and lower breath. Tension in the feet and ankles can creep up through your body and, of course, interfere with good breath and voice work. Even if your feet can't be seen, it doesn't mean they won't affect your voice!

Summary

— Try to discover which communication habits are making it harder for your listeners to hear you. Someone else might help you to identify these. They might also help you to identify your little habits of tension that appear when you are nervous.

— Sustain your voice to the end of each thought or sentence, and talk *to* your listeners, not *at* them. Don't go too fast, and make sure you speak loudly enough to reach the back of the room.

— Look out into the room regularly and make brief eye contact with individuals. Centre your weight for confidence and ease of speaking, and try to move your mouth enough to be understood.

8.

Working with young people

YOUNG PEOPLE WHO LEARN HOW TO USE THEIR VOICE WELL IN THEATRE WORKSHOPS TAKE THESE SKILLS OUT INTO THEIR WORKING LIVES WITH A STRONGER SENSE OF THEIR PLACE IN THE WORLD.

Most of the exercises in this book are suitable for teachers to use when working with young people. However, as I'm sure experienced teachers know, young people – especially adolescents who are becoming self-aware – are likely to be self-conscious and peer-conscious. Try to be sensitive to this as you select voice exercises for your students. It is important that young people don't feel embarrassed about the exercises or the positions they are asked to take. Embarrassment will only lead to physical tensions that will inhibit good voice use.

When I lead young people in voice exercises, I try to place them in a formation that avoids easy eye contact and observation by fellow students. So the circle is not always useful until they feel secure in the work. If you ask students to bend over, it helps to make sure that they don't have anyone behind them. Shaking the body can also be embarrassing and perhaps uncomfortable for girls.

It is a good idea to address the issue of the 'pitch break' (see Exercise 5), which will be most noticeable and probably embarrassing for the boys. When you ask them to slide through the voice on a hum or open vowel, I suggest you tell them all not to be too loud, and tell the boys not to go too high (see Exercises 39 and 45). Boys' voices take some time to settle down after they have 'broken'. If this has happened recently, they don't need to go above the pitch break. If they do, reassure them that it is OK to make the funny noise – and perhaps teach them to yodel!

You will get best results if you demonstrate the exercises first. Give simple, strong instructions, with desired outcomes.

Breath

Explain to your students how actors achieve the feeling of breathing and speaking from their abdomen, and why it matters. I suggest you follow the work in Chapter 1, especially the sections 'How your breath works', 'Touch it' and 'Try it'. Depending on the age of your students, you could also share with them the section 'How your voice works – making sound', including 'How tension restricts your voice'.

<u>Preparation – stretching and releasing</u>
Ask the students to have a good yawn and stretch out their upper body in any way that feels good.

Ask them to shake out their hands and arms, feet and legs.

Exercise 35: Learning some breath control

Your students could do the next two exercises standing up, but young people easily tire and lose good posture. I usually sit them down.

Ask the students to sit upright, but comfortably, in a chair or on the floor with their back against a wall.

Ask them to massage their jaw muscles, face and neck.

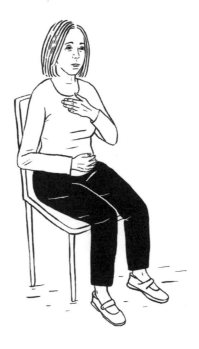

Now ask them to place one hand on their abdomen, where their navel is, to feel the movement of the breath there.
Suggest they think of breathing into this area.
Ask them to place their other hand on their upper chest, and to try not to let the breath push up there.

The teacher should lead the counting on this exercise.

Ask the students to breathe in and then blow the breath out slowly to a count of 10:
then again for a count of 12
then again for a count of 14

then again for a count of 16 (if they can do it without tightening the throat at the end).

––––

You will have to judge how far the students can reasonably go according to their age and size. Small bodies may not go very far, so you could start at six or eight and build up from there.

The students should be encouraged to think of the air coming from their abdomen, not their throat. They will be able to notice the areas under their hands (especially the lower hand) slowly coming in as the air goes out, and then expanding again as they breathe in.

Exercise 36: Speaking from your abdomen

––––

Repeat Exercise 35 but ask the students to count aloud instead of blowing.

Suggest they imagine that their mouth goes right down to the bottom of their abdomen and that they can speak from there. Make sure they know that this doesn't mean their voice has to be deep.

––––

Summary

— Take some time to explain to your students how breathing works.
— Stretch the upper body and release tension to allow the breath and voice to flow easily.
— Use the breathing exercises for your students to develop breath control and to learn to breathe and speak from low in their body.
— Make sure the students don't think that breathing low means speaking with a low pitch.

ALLOW THE FEELING OF YOUR SPEAKING VOICE TO COME FROM YOUR ABDOMEN. YOU COULD IMAGINE THAT YOUR MOUTH GOES RIGHT DOWN TO THERE.

Resonance

In Chapter 2 I described resonance. It would be a good idea to explain it to your students before they try Exercises 37, 38 and 39.

The students could remain seated for these exercises, but they will have more energy if you get them up on to their feet at some point. Then ask them to centre themselves, standing with their weight evenly balanced across their feet. Make sure their knees are not locked.

Exercise 37: Feeling resonance in your chest

———

Ask the students to place a hand on their chest and start humming on long breaths.

Then gently to bang or rub their chest to release more resonance or buzz there.
Ask them to change notes each time they breathe in.

———

Exercise 38: Releasing your voice forward

The next exercise is to help the students to feel the resonance forward at the front of their face and so help audibility.

———

Ask the students to cup their hands together and place them in front of their face, but not touching it.
Then ask them to hum into their hands as if they are catching the resonance in them. They may not actually feel the resonance in their hands – more likely in their face, especially their lips.

Repeat on several different notes. Ask them if they can feel the resonance in their face.

Now ask them to count aloud from one to ten, with the same

sense of catching the resonance of their voice in their hands. They don't have to do this on just one breath.

Ask them to drop their hands, then count to ten again and see if they can still feel resonance at the front of their face.

———

Exercise 39: Playing with resonance

This exercise is to feel resonance through the whole range of the voice.

———

Ask the students to hum and slide their voice around: up and down and all over the place, playing with the range of their voice. Tell the boys not to worry if they hear the pitch break.
Remind them to think the buzz of the resonance into the front of their face and body.

———

Summary

— Take time to explain to your students what resonance is.
— Touching, rubbing and firmly patting the chest releases resonance.
— Use the hands cupped around the face to place resonance forward in the face.
— Slide the voice up and down playfully to feel resonance throughout the range.

Opening the voice

Rib stretches

If the students have been sitting, ask them to stand up and centre themselves by standing with their weight evenly balanced across their feet. Make sure their knees are not locked back.

Ask them to stretch over to one side with their arm over their head, and breathe into the stretched side of their ribs.

Now ask them to stand up straight again, take a breath and feel the difference.

Repeat the stretch on the other side.

Throat stretches

Yawning
Yawning is a great way for the students to stretch all the areas involved with speech: the throat, tongue, lips and face muscles.

Ask them to stretch their body in response to the yawn so they can open up the ribs and shoulders as well.

Stifled yawn
Ask the students to try another yawn, but this time not to open their mouth – as if they were trying to stifle the yawn. Do they feel that big stretch at the back of their mouth?

Exercise 40: Sustained sounds

——

Ask the students to focus on a spot across the room. Now ask them to breathe in and release a long, slow **Mah** to that spot on a comfortable middle note.

They need to use enough vocal energy, but they mustn't push the voice out. You will be able to hear if they do. It will sound forced.

Repeat on a different note, but this time ask them to feel the resonance in their face.

Then ask the students to pretend to take the sound from their mouth with their finger and thumb. Ask them to draw it out and away across the room, getting louder and louder. Make sure they don't start to push or shout in order to be loud. Ask them not to let the voice sound harsh or forced.
Remind them to think of the voice as coming from the abdomen, not the throat.
They can continue this exercise as long as you feel is helpful. Encourage them to listen to and enjoy the sound of their voice.

——

Exercise 41: A sound bath

This is an exercise taught me by my first teacher, David Carey. I suggest it is most suitable for a group of young people who are quite confident and used to working together. Then it will be an extraordinary experience for them.

——

Stand the students in a circle, shoulder to shoulder. If it feels right, ask them to put their arms around the people on either side.

You now need to explain to them what they will be doing, as once they start you won't want to interrupt.
It is best if they close their eyes, but if they don't feel safe like that, then suggest that they look at a spot on the floor at the centre of the circle.

Ask them to focus on their low breathing.

Then ask them to begin by humming on any comfortable note, taking a breath whenever they need to. Suggest they listen to the sound of the whole group together.

Next, when they feel like it (or you could start) they should change the hum to a **Mah** and then continue making long **Mah** sounds.

Tell them they can change their note any time they like. Suggest that they listen to the sound in the circle and add their voice to it in any way that feels right to them. They could change the vowel, add consonants and even harmonise with the other voices.

This is the core of the exercise: to improvise freely with the sounds. The students are not competing with each other but are in harmony: listening, offering and responding. You should emphasise that they shouldn't try to show off as it will break the group experience. If they submit to the group sound they may find they make sounds that surprise them.

In this group experience they are being very creative with their voices: extending them, sharing them and warming them up at the same time, without effort.

If you are in the circle, you should gently pull out and close it behind you once they appear to be committing to the experience.

Finally, each student should step into the centre of the circle, one at a time, and spend some time there without using their own voice but bathed in the voices of the others. You will probably have to direct this. Explain at the beginning of the exercise what is to happen at this stage, telling them that they should stay in the middle for only a minute or two. Then when you feel the sound is going well, gently signal to each student by tapping their shoulder when it is their time to go into the circle.

You should try it too. It is an amazing experience.

———

GOOD ARTICULATION IS ESSENTIAL FOR YOUNG PEOPLE WHO ARE TRYING TO ACHIEVE CLEAR SPEECH WHEN PERFORMING.

Exercise 42: Counting across the space

If the students have just done a sound bath, ask them to return to a place in the room on their own. They are now going to move from open vowel sounds to speaking words.

Ask them to centre their weight again and breathe from their abdomen.
Focus on a spot across the room.

Intoning
Ask them to choose a comfortable middle note (or give them one yourself) and gently hum on it.

Then ask them to breathe in again and count from one to ten, staying on that note and trying to send the words to the spot they are looking at.

Show them what you mean, making sure you stay on the note without the rise and fall of normal speech or 'scooping up' to the note. Exercises 25 to 27 tell you more about intoning.
The students should try to think of the voice flowing away from them across the room.

Ask them to repeat this two or three times, using a different note if they like.

Then ask them to count again quite loudly, this time in normal speech but with the same feeling of the voice flowing across the room.

Exercise 43: Freeing your voice with movement

This exercise frees up the sound and also helps the students to sustain vocal energy.

Ask them to stand with their feet apart, one foot in front of the other. If the left foot is in front, ask them to circle the right arm as if they are throwing a ball. Ask them to imagine that instead of a ball they are throwing their shoulder forward across the room. Put the other foot forward and change arms.
Do four or five circles on each side.

Ask them to do this circling again but this time count to ten at the same time, imagining their voice is being thrown across the room with their shoulder.

Then ask them to repeat the counting to ten without the arm circling but with the memory of releasing the voice across the room.

Then ask them to count again, but circling the arm and throwing the shoulder only on the first and last number.

Ask them to do both these exercises again, speaking lines from their play a phrase or line at a time.

––––

The first part of the exercise helps them to release vocal energy throughout a line or thought. The second helps them to experience vocal energy at the beginning and ends of lines or thoughts. Rushing the beginning of a thought and then letting the energy drop at the end is very common in the speech of inexperienced or untrained actors.
    I suggest you use these shoulder-circling exercises in moderation as they can be tiring.

Exercise 44: A ball game

This exercise is also to help the students to realise that they must keep their vocal energy going to the end of sentences.

––––

If you have two or more students speaking dialogue in a scene, give them a ball and ask them to speak their line and throw the

ball to the next person to speak *as they say the last word of their line.*
This should continue throughout the scene, with each person throwing the ball as they say the last word of their line.
The exercise also helps them to listen to what the other person is saying as they wait to receive the ball.

Then repeat the scene without the ball-throwing but with the memory of sending the last word to the next speaker. Make sure they don't exaggerate this; just sustain the vocal energy in the word.

Now try the whole exercise again, this time throwing a ball on the first word of the line as well as the last word. You will need to use two balls.

Exercise 45: Sliding through your voice

This exercise helps to open out and increase the range of the voice.

Ask the students to centre their weight again and breathe from their abdomen.
Focus on a spot across the room.

Now ask them to slide down through the voice on **Hah** a few times, starting as high and ending as low as they can comfortably manage. Ask them to send the sound up and out across the room, and imagine it landing on their focal point.

Now ask them to slide down on other vowels: **Hey, Hoh, Hee, Haw, How.**
Girls should start this exercise high in the voice, but boys needn't go above their pitch break. However, you should listen out in case they are straining at the top of their speaking voices. Tell them not to go too loud.

Summary

- Side stretches open the ribs, and yawning and stifled yawns open the throat.
- Use a long, sustained **Mah** for your students to feel their voice leave their body.
- The Sound Bath is an enjoyable way of playing with the voice in a group. It also warms and opens the voice.
- Intoning takes open vowel sounds into speech.
- Use movement and ball games for students to send their voices across a space and to each other.
- Sliding down from high notes to low notes helps to increase the range of the voice.

Articulation and words

Understanding and using good articulation is essential for young people who are trying to achieve clear speech when performing. Using the work in the section 'How your voice works – making words' (Chapter 1), let them explore where consonants are made in the mouth with the tongue and the lips.

When working with young people I do a lot of work on consonants and clarity of speech. However, I think it is important that they don't feel there is one accent or one way of pronouncing words that is better than any other.

Actors and student actors may use various accents for characters coming from different regions or countries. They may also be asked to speak in Standard English, too, if a part requires it. Actors who are training learn Standard English as an important tool. But all accents need to be clear and articulate for audiences to understand them.

If young people learn to develop the full potential and clarity of their own voice, in their own accent, they will maintain their authenticity whatever accent they have to use for a role. They do have to understand that it won't be exactly as if they are speaking casually to their friends, because they have to project their authentic voices. They will be opening their mouths more and putting more energy into the words. Then they will be able to share their voices and the words and feelings of their character with their audience.

Exercise 46: Consonant practice

Choose some consonants and repeat in a series: **D,D,D,D K,K,K,K B,B,B,B**. Pick (or ask the students to pick) a variety of them to exercise the tip of the tongue, the back of the tongue, and the lips and teeth.

Then take that work into words with the tongue twisters (Exercise 28). Ask them to try to make all the consonants clear, especially at the ends of words.

They can have fun trying to repeat them very fast, but they must be accurate.

Exercise 47: Exploring the shapes, sounds and energy of words

These exercises with text are for the students to explore words physically in their mouths. Encourage them to think of words as having energy that they can control. They could use a text they are working on or you could give them a poem.

Ask the students to speak the text, mouthing the words silently. This will help them to feel the shapes of the words in their mouth.

Now ask them to whisper the text, being careful not to push the sounds in their throat. This will make them aware of the energy of the consonants as they feel the breath passing through them.

Ask them to speak the text quietly, keeping the sound forward and out. Remind them to think the voice forward into their face, feeling the resonance there. They could cup their hands in front of their face to catch the buzz.

Finally, ask them to speak the text at the right volume for the room you are working in.

Summary

— While clear speech is essential for theatre, explain to your students that it doesn't mean a special way of pronouncing words. All accents can be clear and still be authentic.
— Repeated consonants exercise the tongue.
— Silent speech, whispering and a quiet voice helps students to recognise the physical aspects of speech in the mouth.

A warm-up for young people

Because young people are not always confident about their growing bodies and changing voices, the physical and vocal rigours of voice warm-ups can be a challenge. So I've brought together exercises to form a structured warm-up that will allow them to feel comfortable as well as help them to speak loudly and clearly, with plenty of variety in their voice. This warm-up should take 15 to 30 minutes. I suggest you work thoroughly through the exercises in this chapter with the students before you use the warm-up.

Preparation stretches
Ask the students to have a good yawn and stretch out their upper body in any way that feels good.

Ask them to move their face muscles around: stretching, scrunching up and pulling funny faces.

Now ask them to massage their face and jaw.

Breath

In this exercise the teacher should lead the counting.

Ask the students to sit upright but comfortably in a chair or on the floor with their back against a wall. Alternatively, they could stand with their weight centred and their knees soft.

Ask them to breathe from their abdomen.

Ask them to breathe in and then blow the breath out slowly to a count of 10.
Then ask them to do it again for a count of 12.
Then again for a count of 14.
Then again for a count of 16 (if they can).
Ask them to think of the air coming from their abdomen, not their throat.

Ask them to notice their ribs coming down and their abdominal muscles coming in as the air goes out.

Resonance

Ask the students to hum into their chest and feel the buzz of the resonance with their hands.

Now ask them to gently bang or rub their chest to release more resonance.
They should change notes each time they breathe in.

Placing the voice forward
Ask them to place their hands in front of their face and hum into them. Ask them to imagine catching the resonance with their hands.

Repeat on several different notes.

Ask them to count aloud from one to ten, with the same sense of catching the resonance of their voice in their hands.

Ask them to drop their hands and count to ten again, and see if they can still feel resonance at the front of their faces.

Now ask them to hum and slide the voice around: up and down, and all over the place, playing with the range of the voice.
Remind the boys not to worry if they hear the pitch break.

Suggest they try to feel the buzz of the resonance forward in their face and body.

Sustained sounds
Ask them to start on a gentle hum, then release long, sustained vowels across the space.
Take one vowel per breath, and ask the students to think the sound from their abdomen, not their throat, and to focus it on a spot across the room.
Change note for each new breath.

<u>Intoning</u>

Now ask them to intone counting or some text on one note with the same sense of releasing sounds across the space. Make sure that the students breathe into their abdomen and think their voice from there each time.

Repeat, speaking normally, with the same sense of releasing the voice across the space. Again, the students should breathe into their abdomen and think their voice out from there.

Articulation and words

Use any repeated consonants and vowels, exercising the tip of the tongue, the back of the tongue, and the lips and teeth.

Practise some tongue twisters.

<u>Text</u>

It is a good idea to end a voice warm-up with a piece of text, either the words of their play or perhaps a suitable poem. Choose from the following exercises:

Ask the students to mouth the words without sound, then to whisper them.
Then ask them to speak them quietly, and finally to speak them loud enough for their performance space.

Facing the front, ask the students to circle one arm and at the same time speak the words. They should imagine they are throwing the words forward across the space with their shoulder. Alternatively they could circle the arm and throw just the first and last words of each phrase or line.

Ask the students to intone the words across the space, feeling the energy flow away from them.
Then ask them to speak the words normally, but with the same feeling of the voice flowing across the space.

9.

Voice work at the National Theatre

GOOD BREATH AND VOICE WORK
CAN MAKE A BETTER ACTOR.

As you work with this book, it may inspire you to remember that many of our greatest actors are doing exactly the same exercises.

Working with actors

Why do actors need a voice coach?

People sometimes ask me why professional actors need a voice coach. My answer is usually to compare my role to that of an athletics coach. Primarily, I keep trained actors' voices in shape in order to meet the demands of their job, but I can also help them to keep improving their vocal technique. Athletes, singers and dancers all continue to work on their technique throughout their career, so why shouldn't actors?

At the National Theatre we have two of the largest and most demanding theatres in the country. Most of the actors I work with here have had some sort of training – but not all. My responsibility to both the National Theatre and the actors is to make sure that they are audible and clear. The challenge is to enable them to be heard properly while maintaining character and truthfully conveying stories to audiences used to the intimacy of film and television.

Voice work in large theatres

It is not just audiences who are affected by film and TV; actors are too. Young actors can be particularly concerned about being truthful and real when acting in large theatres. Earlier generations were able to continue their training in weekly repertory theatres, where they had the chance to play lots of roles in a reasonably big theatre over a season. That system has long gone, and the experience young actors have at drama school today will be mainly in small theatres or studio-type venues. Following that, their first few jobs might be in television or film.

Here at the National Theatre I have begun a scheme to help young actors to practise filling large theatre spaces with their voices. Each year we invite the country's principal drama schools to bring their students, with their voice teachers, to spend time in our Olivier theatre. This theatre is based on a Greek amphitheatre, so it is especially large and wide, with the audience fanning out in front of the stage. Young actors are always surprised at how much energy and volume they have to use to fill every corner of the auditorium. They also discover that speech that seems to be very loud and perhaps over-pronounced to them on the stage sounds perfectly natural to the audience in the auditorium. Consonants are particularly important, as they are the sounds that most easily get lost.

The apron (the front part) of the Olivier stage is thrust a little into the auditorium. Therefore, as the actor comes down on to it, some of the audience are behind them, and if they turn to the side, even more of the audience are behind them. This means that they have to be particularly careful not to drop their vocal energy at the ends of their words and phrases, or these can be lost from the ear of the audience behind them.

The bulk of the stage is a big circle that reaches far back, away from the audience, with a huge tower above into which scenery is flown. Such a big theatre demands superb vocal technique in order to present drama that is epic and powerful yet modern and acceptable to audiences today. Giving young actors a chance to experience such a theatre is proving to be very positive. The students and teachers have risen to its challenges, and this is helping to bridge the gap between their training and the professional stage. We can't complain about young actors not being able to fill the spaces with their voices if we don't give them a chance to practise!

'Match fitness'

Most actors find that their work varies between theatre, television, film and perhaps radio. Therefore they might come to the National Theatre not having worked in a theatre for some time. My job then is to get them back to 'match fitness': to rediscover the technique, stamina and confidence to work easily and flexibly in our big theatre spaces.

As I have shown you in this book, speaking is a very physical activity. This means that speaking professionally in big theatres can be athletic and often emotionally demanding work. It is an intense experience, and needs an enormous amount of energy for each performance. If an actor has been away from the theatre for some time and tries to go into a play without getting their voice back into shape, the voice gets very tired.

At the National Theatre, plays are mostly in a repertory system, which means that one play alternates every four or five days with another play. Often the actors are also rehearsing a new play during the day. In most other theatres, actors will do eight shows a week (six evening performances and two matinees). Length of run varies, but actors can often be contracted for a year at a time. So you can see that being a good theatre actor takes great stamina.

Besides the technical aspects of performing, actors regularly have to deal with anxiety and fear, which affect their breathing and therefore their voice. There are many good reasons for them to feel these emotions. They might be anxious about pleasing the play's director. They might worry about working easily with a new company of actors. They might be concerned about their vocal ability or remembering lines (especially as they get older). Above all, they might be simply concerned about getting it right and being good enough in a profession where they are constantly and publicly judged on their work.

You may think the more experienced or successful actors would not feel like this. But when performers are at the top of their game the stakes just get higher. I have to remind *them* to breathe also.

How I work

I always begin with breathing exercises, helping actors to reconnect with the technique of breathing deeply, freely and frequently enough to carry the voice with ease. Actors soon learn that the better their breath-work, the more truthful their voices sound. Good breath and voice work can make a better actor. Every pre-performance vocal warm-up I lead with a company of actors begins with breathing.

Organising the breathing also helps with performance anxiety. If an actor is getting very nervous in the wings before going on stage, I will suggest that they do the hand-pressing exercise (Exercise 30). As they press the heels of the hands together, the pelvic floor muscles are activated, supporting low breathing and allowing the upper body to relax and release. This exercise also helps them to focus and 'be in the moment' rather than fearing what is to come.

I use the exercises in this book with all actors but I also tailor them to the specific needs of the play and the character. For example, when we are exploring how a particular character speaks, we might consider whether they use a particular type of vocal resonance. To do this, we might experiment by speaking from different parts of the body, just as you did in Exercise 3. This can subtly change the quality of the voice, and makes you feel different too.

If an actor is pushing or forcing their voice, I often suggest that they explore the feeling of breathing into the ribs at the lower back and then imagining that their voice comes from there. This heightens their sense of the voice coming from deep in their body, and stops them from using too much effort in the throat or face.

Working with directors

The greatest privilege I have is to listen. I spend a good deal of my time in the rehearsal rooms watching and listening to directors and actors. My understanding of the director's vision for the play is crucial to my working processes. I have to engross myself in the world of the play almost as much as the actors do.

How I work

The words of the play are not always the first priority with actors or directors. In the early part of rehearsals, as they begin to find the reality of their character, most actors will be exploring the sub-text of the play. This is the space between the words that allows the actor to use their creative imagination to discover what is being thought rather than said.

In this early stage the words are often not spoken very clearly or forcefully. Some actors and directors like this place very much and can find it hard to move from it into the text itself. Sometimes part of my job is to remind them that the story they have chosen to tell needs to be released through the words, and that the energy of the language carries the energy of the character's (and the play's) thoughts and ideas.

Some directors concentrate on the physical aspects of the play and the characters, creating the scenes and telling the stories through improvisation and movement – often with thrilling results. In this type of production, my job is to help the actors to bring language into that physical world and avoid the words being overwhelmed by their physicality. I might work on the rhetoric of the piece, drawing attention to the way their character structures thoughts and chooses vocabulary. I would also remind them of the need for clear and muscular articulation. Of course, I would have to do that work without contradicting the style of the direction.

Other directors are most interested in 'blocking' the action: placing the actors in the set and telling the story through precisely chosen moves. In this type of production, I would use plenty of movement in my exercises in order for the actors to experience the language of the play in a physical way. My aim would be to remind them that speech is itself physical and that movement can release the meaning of words.

Then there are directors who are extremely interested in language and spend time with the actors considering how each character's thoughts and actions are channelled through their words. In this type of production, I would support that process with good voice workouts, making sure the actors have the breath and voice to carry the language.

I have to get to know the actors too: how they work and how they use their voices. I take nothing for granted. Even if I've worked with an actor many times before, each new play is a fresh start for all of us, with different and particular demands.

I HAVE YET TO MEET AN ACTOR
WHO DOESN'T WANT TO BE HEARD.

When I work

So I listen to the director and I listen to the actors. By doing so I find out what work I need to do and when to do it. Timing is important because I need to gauge when individual actors are ready for my input. Some don't want to think about their voice early on in rehearsals, whereas others want to work with me from the beginning.

Directors can be the same and have strong opinions as to when it is appropriate for their company of actors to begin to think about audibility and clarity. Sometimes a director wants me to take the whole company on to the stage early in the rehearsal period to get a sense of the size they will have to play. Another might be concerned that thinking too big too soon will destroy the truthfulness of the acting. Others will not be concerned about voice work at all, leaving it entirely to me to decide how to work with the actors when they are free from rehearsal.

Occasionally directors feel that voice work is unnecessary, believing that once actors are trained they shouldn't need any more assistance from a voice teacher. And some directors can have concerns that my input might interfere with their creative vision for the play. These responses are valid, and I have to find ways to reassure those directors of my integrity and experience.

The solution usually comes from the actors themselves. Most actors are pleased to use the expertise of an experienced theatre voice coach, and having worked for so many years in British theatre I know many of our actors well. As you will have seen from this book, the work is about personal development, and many actors really love this aspect of their craft. It is only in our big repertory theatres that they can work with a resident coach and get the opportunity to move their work forward. They know that keeping their voice in shape helps them to grow as actors, as it increases their flexibility and gives them confidence in their vocal and therefore acting abilities.

The final part of my job is in the theatre itself during the technical rehearsal of the play and the preview performances. Then I sit in different parts of the auditorium to check that the actors can be heard clearly everywhere. The actors themselves seek reassurance about their audibility – I have yet to meet an actor who doesn't want to be heard.

So my job requires sensitivity and skill, as building relationships with directors and actors is vital. I am not there to change actors' voices: they are cast for who they are and what they can do. Nor should I impose my interpretation of character or language upon an actor. I am there to help them achieve their full potential. Producing great theatre is a team effort and I have to be ready to work how and when I'm needed. Job satisfaction, however, is enormous. It is a privilege to be able to work with great actors and to assist them in making great art.

ON THE STAGES OF THE NATIONAL
THEATRE, ACTORS ALWAYS TRY TO
SPEAK WITH WELL-SUPPORTED VOICES.

Conclusion

VOICE TRAINING IS
EMPOWERING AND LIBERATING.

When we work with voice and communication skills, we must first consider the voice itself and how we produce it, and then the use of voice in producing speech. Both elements are equally important and inextricably intertwined. For words to affect a listener or persuade them of their validity or truth, they need to be carried on a voice that is not only clear and easy but also authentic and 'owned' by the speaker.

In the long run it will not help you to try to manufacture a sound. The work is not about faking it or trying to sound like someone else. It is about getting to know and falling in love with the voice you have. Then you will be able to express who you are and share the stories you want to tell, clearly and easily. We all have the potential to use our voice well. Our voice can become more resonant and truly expressive. We can give it more energy through better breathing habits and more precise articulation. Most important of all, our voice can feel and sound more comfortable and honest.

As you get to know your voice and learn to control it, you will increasingly feel how good it is to sound like you. This will give you confidence in whatever 'role' you have to play in your work. By this I don't mean pretending, even if your work is acting. Just as a well-trained actor brings honesty and truthfulness to a character and situation, so your voice will be authentic in whatever situation you use it.

The work in this book is about your voice and your personal development. Even if you are a teacher whose primary aim is to help your students to use their voices effectively, you need to know the work yourself with your own voice and body. As a teacher, you will be well aware of the great demands regularly put on your voice. So as you get to know the work for your students, you also learn how to use your own voice well, and how to keep it healthy and strong.

And it is work. The voice is physical and there is no 'quick fix' for effective physical change. It takes time and thought: first to learn how your voice works, then to explore and experience that in yourself, then to put the techniques into practice and feel the progress in your voice and breathing.

The techniques I use for actors can be practised by anyone who uses their voice as part of their work. It is not surprising that in recent years the commercial sector and other professions have started to recognise the importance of investing in the voice and communication skills of employees. They recognise that they can learn from the training of modern actors. They realise that the skills, techniques and disciplines that actors use to produce truthful, moving and persuasive characters can be incredibly valuable to their organisations. Voice, of course, is at the forefront of communication skills, and theatre voice trainers are increasingly being invited to share their skills with people from other professions.

Voice training is empowering and liberating. It teaches self-awareness and leads to eloquent self-expression and self-confidence. This confidence can go on to affect people's entire lives, well beyond the environment for which the training is first required. Young people, in particular, who learn how to use their voice well in theatre workshops and for student productions, take these skills out into their working lives with a stronger sense of their place in the world.

Actors learn that knowing how to use their voice well gives them confidence in their acting, and most recognise the value of ongoing training. Those who trained their voices at drama school still need to keep them in shape and perhaps develop them further. If they have been working away from the theatre, they need to get back to 'match fitness' when they return. Then they also need to warm up their voices for every performance.

If our voice is an important part of our work – whether we are actors, teachers, business people, lawyers, lecturers, faith group leaders, sales people, call-centre workers, fundraisers or therapists – we will gain great confidence from understanding our voice, developing a relationship with it, looking after it and learning how to use it well. So it's over to you. Kick off your shoes, have a good stretch and get down to work.

WE ALL HAVE THE POTENTIAL
TO USE OUR VOICE WELL.

Index